Baby Names

Eleanor Turner

2014

white
LADDER

Acknowledgements

I would like to extend my utmost gratitude to Cerys Owen, Shelley Heck and Michael Turner for their contributions; without them this book would have been much shorter. My thanks are also given to Beth Bishop at Crimson Publishing for her patience and guidance throughout the project. Finally, the greatest thanks go to my children, Owen Henri and Jasper Hugh. I fall more in love with them, and their names, every day.

This third edition published by Crimson Publishing in 2013.

ISBN: 978 1 90828 160 9

Typeset by IDSUK (DataConnection) Ltd

Printed and bound in the United States of America by Sheridan Books Inc, Michigan

Contents

A note on how to use this book

While the author and publisher acknowledge that baby names vary widely in spelling and pronunciation, this book lists each name only once: under the most common initial and spelling. If a name has an alternate spelling with a different initial, it may be listed under that letter also.

Information relating to statistics and trends in baby names is based on the most recent data at the time of going to press.

Introduction

Did you know that the name Aaliyah is amongst the most popular names in New Mexico, but not in any other state?

Do you know why Queen Elizabeth II is allowed a say in royal baby names?

Have you noticed the trend for military names recently, including Major, Gunner, and Archer?

As daunting as it might sound at first, choosing a name for your baby is one of the most enjoyable, often hilarious, and best decisions you get to make as a new parent. You are being given free rein to get as creative as possible, to honor a family member or celebrity you love, or to find meaning in the dozens of names you've loved over the years. Who doesn't like the sound of that?

However, baby-naming is not without its pitfalls. Sometimes choosing the right name is simply a case of hearing one you like and knowing instantly that you've chosen correctly. But for some parents the naming game gets far more complicated when they start trying to please parents, grandparents, friends, and siblings, while simultaneously trying to avoid names that could be shortened into ridiculous nicknames or would make for funny initials.

And here's another thing: you'll probably want to choose something unique, but not *too* unique, or something common, but not *too* common. A name could be inspired by an admired celebrity, a sports star, or an influential historical or political figure. It could come from the family tree, or follow a current baby-naming trend. You also need to make sure you love it—you and your baby will have to live with it forever! The possibilities are endless so it's understandable that it can set some parents into panic mode.

Well, never fear. *Baby Names 2014* is here to take you through your options and solve your baby-naming dilemmas. It's updated annually, so it always includes the year's most popular names, celebrity choices, and names making a comeback. We've included dozens of lists to provide you with inspiration, and, of course, some downright kooky names children have been given over the years (usually by celebrities).

Take a peek at the most up-to-date trends in baby-naming, from the backlash against eccentric names to the return of the traditional, and some recent celebrity trends. Read about how movie stars and the characters they play influence what we name our children, what teachers *really* think about the names in their classrooms, and what happened to baby name trends when a new Pope was elected last year.

Be sure to keep an eye out for all the facts and figures we've got for you—including what names are most popular around the world—so you can either go with the flow . . . or deliberately go against it.

The average length of a baby name is six letters.

This book is broken into two sections: the first deals with how to figure out what to name your child through a series of questions and suggestions, and the second gives you a meaning for each name you're considering. There's no right or wrong way to use this book, just as there's no right or wrong way to make your baby-naming decision.

Remember, picking a baby name should be fun! Grab a pencil, dip in, and find some names you like. Use the tons of suggestions we've given you to work out if one of them is your baby's new name.

Good luck!

part one

1

What was hot in 2013?

The reign of eccentric names

Have you ever raised your eyebrows when you heard a friend's baby name choice? Statistics say you probably have.

Research shows that we are seeing more variation in the names parents are choosing than ever before. In the 1950s, the Top 25 boys' names and the Top 50 girls' names were given to 50% of all babies born in that decade. To reach the same figure now, you would have to include the Top 147 boys' names and the Top 327 girls'. This means that there is a far greater variety of names, spellings, pronunciations, and contracted names than ever before.

One explanation for this is that parents have begun to give their child a name *more* unusual than their own. A parent who has enjoyed their slightly unusual name will feel more confident about giving their offspring an even more unique name. This has been a rising trend since the 1990s, which would make sense, as children who were born in the early 1990s with eccentric names are now having children themselves. If this trend continues into 2014 and beyond, you can be sure that names will get stranger and stranger . . .

Some of the US's quirky baby names during the last year have included Driver, Jvier, Mats, and Zkai for boys, and Dulce, Greysi, Poetry, and Pink for girls.

Traditional names continue to impress

What's interesting about recent trends, however, is that no matter how many new and unusual names enter the most popular baby name lists each year, you will always see a large number of babies given the same familiar and traditional names of the past. The Top 10 names for both boys and girls seem to stay pretty fixed each year, and 2013 was no different.

The names Jacob, Ethan, and Michael have appeared in the Top 10 boys' names every year since 2002, and the girls' names Sophia, Isabella, and Emma have also stayed put. As always there was shuffling in the ranks, but the only newcomers last year were Liam for the boys and Elizabeth for the girls, pushing Daniel and Chloe both down to 11th place.

Incredibly, either Jacob or Michael has remained the top choice for parents of newborn baby boys in the US for the last 60 years. While Jacob may have been given to more babies (4.85 million and counting), Michael has claimed the top spot more often (44 times). Jacob has now been in the top spot for an astonishing 14 years in a row.

Top 10 baby boy names

1. Jacob
2. Mason
3. Ethan
4. Noah
5. William

6. Liam
7. Jayden
8. Michael
9. Alexander
10. Aiden

Top 10 baby girl names

1. Sophia
2. Emma
3. Isabella
4. Olivia
5. Ava

6. Emily
7. Abigail
8. Mia
9. Madison
10. Elizabeth

Liam was the only new name among the Top 10 for boys, and Elizabeth the only new name for girls.

We've also seen traditional names re-enter the charts, and a wonderful example of this is the name Charlotte. Once a consistently popular name in the US, usually appearing in the Top 50 from 1913 to 1953, it had dropped to 309th place by 1982. However, in the last decade it's seen a massive increase in use, and last year clawed its way back to position 19. If this trend continues, next year it will enter the Top 10 for the first time ever. In fact, Charlotte has now become so fashionable again that even shortened versions of it are gaining momentum: Charlie entered the Top 1,000 for baby girls in 2005 and in just seven years has leaped over 600 places to position 305. It's also remaining a steady favorite for parents of little boys, as the same name has climbed just over 200 spots in the last decade in the boys' charts.

More traditional names had dropped out of mainstream use by the 1980s and become vastly unpopular, but in the last few years names ending in -a, -ie, and -en have started to see a resurgence, particularly as a spelling option for parents who like the sound of a traditional name but want to give it a modern twist. Just take a look at the Top 10 (six of the names for baby girls end in -a), or the highest-climbers (five of the 10 biggest climbers also end in -a). Other old-fashioned names, such as Henry, Jasper, Hannah, Marilyn, and William, have climbed the popularity ranks in the Top 100 lists, along with their alternate spelling options of Henri, Jaz, Hanna, Mae, and Will.

The traditional name for baby boys in some Christian families has often been Noah, which has now become so popular in the US that it entered the Top 10 for the first time in 2009 and last year appeared in fourth place. That's an amazing jump of over 200 places since 1992.

2013 popular newcomers

Boys	Girls
Ari	Arya
Brantley	Briella
Gael	Cataline
Iker	Elisa
Jase	Haven
King	Marilyn
Major	Perla
Maverick	Raelyn
Messiah	Raelynn
Noble	Rosalie

Atten-tion!

One fascinating trend last year was the increase in military names—particularly for baby boys. In fact, of the hundreds of names to show large jumps in popularity, military names made up a significant proportion. The name Major leapt over 500 places from 2012 to 2013, by far the biggest climber of the year, followed by Maverick (thanks, *Top Gun*), King, Gunnar, Gunner, Archer, and Colt. One theory about this is the effect of war. As wars in the Middle East continue to dominate the media and families are separated by military service, it's entirely possible that new parents turn to military-themed names as a way to pay tribute to those serving the nation. Acting Commissioner Colvin said of the trend: "I have no doubt Major's rising popularity as

a boy's name is in tribute to the brave members of the US
military, and maybe we'll see more boys named General in
the future." Maybe he's right!

The effects of the
entertainment industry

Characters in TV programs, movies, and books have been
having a huge impact on baby names in the last few years.
In 2013 the film *The Great Gatsby* piqued our interest in
names from a bygone era: the 1920s. Jay, Daisy, Nick,
Myrtle, Tom, and Jordan were starting to become fairly
common names during this century, but many of them
were deeply unfashionable within 40–50 years. However,
names have ways of coming back around after enough
time, and this is certainly true for names from this era. For
example, the name "Jay" doesn't appear anywhere in the
Top 100 names for boys during the 1920s, but "James,"
which Jay is short for, reached third place in 1928. By 1999
it had sunk to 19th place, but it's already back to 14th
place again. This pattern is repeated often: Daisy, the 155th
most popular name for baby girls in 1920, doesn't appear
anywhere on the Top 500 by 1970, but last year it was
right back up again in position 172. This trend is definitely
set to continue, so who knows? Maybe Myrtle will make a
comeback! (Probably not though: it hasn't been seen in the
Top 1,000 since the 1960s.)

The name Elvis dropped out of the Top 1,000 US baby
names in 2010, the first year it had not made the list

since 1954. It appeared briefly in 2011, but has since
disappeared again.

Other movies don't seem to inspire parents as much. *Star
Trek Into Darkness* and *The Hobbit: The Desolation of
Smaug* were both massive box office hits, but parents didn't
seem as keen to choose character names for their babies as
usual. It's extremely likely in these two examples that the
names are just too "out there" for most of us! The name
Kirk, after Captain Kirk, inspired only 96 families to name
their babies that, and as for Bilbo Baggins . . . well . . .

Quvenzhané Wallis, the pint-sized nominee for a
Best Actress Academy Award last year thanks to
her role in *Beasts of the Southern Wild,* has had to
repeatedly explain how to properly pronounce her
name, and where it comes from. A hybrid of her
mother's and father's names (Qulyndreia and Venjie),
with the addition of the Swahili word for fairy (*zhané*),
Quvenzhané was often heard correcting interviewers
during the 2013 awards season.

The movie trilogy based on *The Hunger Games* novels
provided parents with a whole host of alternative spellings
for already popular names. Since the books and movies
were released, the names Peeta and Gale have entered
the boys' names lists for the first time ever. In fact, the
spelling "Gael" is one of the biggest climbers, moving up an
astonishing 350 places in a single year. The name Katniss

was given to 12 baby girls last year (the first time that's happened), and the name Primrose, or "Prim," has started to climb the charts already, which supports the idea that parents are starting to choose old-fashioned names again.

The more unusual names of Rue and Cato have also been adopted by some parents: the name Rue, a small and sympathetic character in the opening installment of the series, was given to 32 baby girls last year, and, rather alarmingly, the name of the cruel, brutal character Cato was given to 13 baby boys.

An Israeli couple have called their baby girl "Like" after the Facebook button. Their other children are called Pie and Vash, which means honey.

Other influential books last year included the runaway success of *Fifty Shades of Grey*—rumored to be released as a film sometime in 2014. The main characters, Anastasia (Ana) and Christian, persuaded many parents to use their names for their babies. Anastasia has jumped 30 places and is only marginally less popular than Ana, and Christian has remained a firm favorite in the Top 50.

Did you know Queen Elizabeth II gets a say in what new princes and princesses are called? In 1988, Princess Beatrice was going to be called Annabel, but the Queen dismissed it as "too yuppie," according to a British newspaper. She suggested the more traditional Beatrice, and it stuck. Maybe she had the final say in Will and Kate's little one too!

TV inspiration

Game of Thrones, HBO's runaway success of a fantasy-world drama based on the George R. R. Martin series of books, has been held accountable for the increase in popularity of the name Arya. Unheard of before 2010, it was the biggest climber for girls' names last year and jumped nearly 300 places. The spelling "Aria" also saw an increase in popularity and appeared in the Top 100 last year for the first time ever.

Downton Abbey continued to impress parents: the name Violet, for example, from Maggie Smith's acerbic character Violet Crawley, the Dowager Countess of Grantham, has proved popular—over 3,500 baby girls were given the name Violet last year.

NBC's second season of *Smash* might be able to claim responsibility for the newest trend of naming your baby Ivy, after one of the leading characters, but it's more likely that Beyoncé and Jay-Z's little girl is the main reason it continues to move up in the charts. However, *Smash* might genuinely be accountable for the sudden interest in the name Marilyn, after its storyline on a Marilyn Monroe Broadway musical: after years of neglect, "Marilyn" suddenly jumped 120 places last year and looks set for a real comeback. Keep reading for more on celebrity naming trends.

Beyoncé might be on to something: Blue Ivy is the sixth celebrity child to be named after the color. Other "blue" parents include Cher, John Travolta, The Edge, Geri Halliwell, and Alicia Silverstone.

Celebrity power

Celebrities are infamous for choosing obscure names for their babies, but last year's birth announcements seemed to be a little more conservative than usual. This trend was helped along by the Duke and Duchess of Cambridge's little boy, Prince George of Cambridge, born in July 2013. We are sure the name George, which means "farmer", will no doubt rocket up the charts this year.

Recent deliveries from the celebrity stork have included some really traditional baby girl names: Natalie (Shiri Appleby), Margot (Sophie Dahl), Wilhelmina (Taylor Hanson), and Marnie Rose (Lily Allen); and the same for boys: Angelo (Adele), Noah (Megan Fox), Felix (Hugh Grant), Sebastian (Amber Rose and Malin Akerman both chose this one), and Mario (Perez Hilton). There was a sprinkling of weird ones too, though (Rocky springs to mind, thanks to Sarah Michelle Gellar . . .), but then it wouldn't be a complete list of celebrity baby names without them!

There's a bit of a trend among celebrity parents at the moment for choosing names of cities or other geographical features: North (Kim Kardashian and Kanye West's daughter), Camden (both Nick Lachey and Kristin Cavallari chose this name for their sons), Milan (Shakira's baby boy), Ava Berlin (Jeremy Renner's daughter), Vivian Lake (Gisele Bündchen's little girl), and Tennessee (Reese Witherspoon's new baby boy) all seem inspired by places their parents have visited and loved. Of course, this is hardly a new trend: the Beckhams were notorious for choosing the name Brooklyn when their eldest son was born in 1999, after announcing that he was conceived in the New York City suburb. Mariah Carey named her son Moroccan in 2011, Chris Hemsworth chose India Rose for his daughter in 2012, and *Girls* actress Jemima Kirke has both daughter Rafaella Israel and son Memphis to add to the list. Other recent geographical names include Adalaide (Katherine Heigl's adopted daughter), Dakota (Rosie O'Donnell's adopted daughter), and Penelope Scotland (Kourtney Kardashian's second child).

Celebrity babies of the last year

Rocky James (Sarah Michelle Gellar and Freddie Prinze Jr.)
Camden John (Nick Lachey and Vanessa Lachey)
Camden Jack (Kristin Cavallari and Jay Cutler)
Felix Chang (Hugh Grant and Tinglan Hong)
Sebastian Taylor Thomaz (Amber Rose and Wiz Khalifa)
Mario Armando Lavandeira (Perez Hilton)
Milan (Shakira and Gerard Piqué)
Magnus (Elizabeth Banks and Max Handelman)
Miranda Scarlett (Rob Schneider and Patricia Schneider)
Fiona Hepler (Chad Lowe and Kim Lowe)
Rainbow Aurora (Holly Madison and Pasquale Rotella)
Lincoln (Kristen Bell and Dax Shepard)
Livingston (Camila Alves McConaughey and Matthew McConaughey)
Vivian Lake (Gisele Bündchen and Tom Brady)
Tennessee James (Reese Witherspoon and Jim Toth)
Dakota (Rosie O'Donnell and Michelle Rounds)

Marnie Rose (Lily Allen and Sam Cooper)
Magnus Hamilton (Jennifer Nettles and Justin Miller)
William Luca (James Marsden and Rose Costa)
Lula Rosylea (Bryan Adams and Alicia Grimaldi)
Elijah Joseph Daniel (Elton John and David Furnish)
Alessandra Linville (Devon Aoki and James Bailey)
Holiday Grace (Harold Perrineau and Brittany Perrineau)
Jett (Lisa Ling and Paul Song)
Kenzie Lynne (Beverley Mitchell and Michael Cameron)
Scout Margery (Kerri Walsh-Jennings and Casey
    Jennings)
Sebastian (Malin Akerman and Roberto Zincone)
Edward (Eva Herzigová and Gregorio Marsiaj)
Everly (Channing Tatum and Jenna Dewan-Tatum)
Marcus Anthony (Josh and Anna Duggar)
North (Kim Kardashian and Kanye West)
Ace Knute (Jessica Simpson and Eric Johnson)
Charlotte (Colin Hanks and Samantha Bryant)
Prince George of Cambridge (Duke and
    Duchess of Cambridge)

A royal appointment

The most anticipated baby name of 2013 was, of course, that of the Duke and Duchess of Cambridge's baby boy George. It was assumed the name would be either a past monarch, or the name of a member of their close family. There was speculation that Will and Kate would choose to honor as many people as possible by giving their baby dozens of names. One suggestion was Alexandra Diana Elizabeth Carole Philippa Victoria for a girl, or Albert Charles Michael Henry James Philip for a boy—both include names from grandparents, parents, and siblings of the couple, as well as a nod to past monarchs. After his birth on 22 July 2013, the couple chose to call their baby boy George Alexander Louis, and announced the name just two days later—quick for royal standards. There have been six British monarchs called George, including the Queen's father, George VI. Alexander is said to have been a favorite of Kate's, and Louis is one of William's middle names. The little prince will be officially known as His Royal Highness Prince George of Cambridge. It will be interesting to see how high these three names climb up the charts this year.

The Queen's full name is Elizabeth Alexandra Mary Windsor.

One way in which celebs are choosing to set their children apart is by giving them multiple first names and actually using them all. Singer/photographer Bryan Adams and his partner Alicia Grimaldi call their new baby girl by her full name, Lula Rosylea, as do Lily Allen and Sam Cooper with their daughter Marnie Rose. Model Devon Aoki uses her daughter's long name too, Alessandra Linville, when introducing her (which is a bit of a mouthful with all those consonants).

Of course, there are always the stars who take trends and just run with them, using not only something wacky but also multiple names when one will do: *Lost* star Harold Perrineau and his wife have recently added a baby girl to the family, and call her Holiday Grace. Pretty, but a bit long and a bit silly. Ex-glamor model Holly Madison also did the same thing with her new addition, Rainbow Aurora. Both families have defended their choices, with one publicly saying:

❝ There are a lot of smug haters out there who bag on my choice of a name, but I don't care about what they think. I want my daughter to be proud of who she is and learn to speak up and stand up for herself at a young age. ❞

Holly Madison

Bizarre celebrity baby names of recent years

Bingham Hawn (Kate Hudson and Matthew Bellamy—also parents to Ryder)

Blue Ivy (Beyoncé Knowles and Jay-Z)

Buddy Bear Maurice (Jools and Jamie Oliver—also parents to Daisy Boo Pamela, Poppy Honey Rosie, and Petal Blossom Rainbow)

Cosima Violet (Claudia Schiffer and Matthew Vaughn—also parents to Caspar and Clementine)

Ever Imre (Alanis Morissette and Mario Treadway)

Harper Seven (Victoria and David Beckham—also
   parents to Brooklyn, Romeo, and Cruz)
Holiday Grace (Harold Perrineau and Brittany Perrineau)
Ikhyd (M.I.A. and Ben Brewer)
Kahekili (Evangeline Lilly and Norman Kalil)
Lion (Alex O'Loughlin and Malia Jones)
Rainbow Aurora (Holly Madison and
   Pasquale Rotella)

Colin Firth doesn't like his name, apparently. He was quoted as saying: "Colin is the sort of name you'd give your goldfish for a joke. I once saw an episode of *Blackadder* with a dachshund in it called Colin. It seemed his name alone was supposed to reduce you to fits of laughter."

State differences

What's interesting about US baby name statistics is that there is such variety in the popularity of names across different states and territories . . .

- The name Gabriel appears as one of the most popular boys' names only in Alaska, while the names Sophia, Isabella, and Emma appear in almost every single Top 5 girls' list in the country.

- While the names William and Liam were popular across the board, only parents in Iowa and Michigan were likely to name their baby boys Carter.

- Baby girls were predominantly given names such as Olivia or Madison, except in New Mexico, where Aaliyah made the Top 5.

The fifth most popular girls' name in the District of Columbia is currently Genesis, even though it was given to only 34 babies.

It seems as though geography can have a major impact on baby-naming decisions, and population density can certainly change the rankings. States with smaller populations, like Wyoming or Vermont, usually have slightly different names making up their Top 5 each year. Wyoming, for example, has Logan and Wyatt listed for baby boys, and Elizabeth for baby girls—and these aren't found in many of the other states listed. The reasoning for this is simple: fewer babies born means each baby name chosen carries greater weight. For Owen to make the fourth spot in Vermont it needed only 37 parents to choose it; to have the same impact in California, it would need over 2,600. Likewise, only 23 babies were called Olivia in Wyoming last year, but it still claimed fifth place.

So find your state from the lists below—and make sure your baby won't have another 10 Isabellas or Jacobs in their class!

Top five girls' names by state

State	Rank 1	Rank 2	Rank 3	Rank 4	Rank 5
Alabama	Emma	Ava	Olivia	Isabella	Madison
Alaska	Emma	Sophia	Olivia	Abigail	Ava
Arizona	Sophia	Isabella	Emma	Mia	Olivia
Arkansas	Emma	Sophia	Ava	Isabella	Olivia
California	Sophia	Isabella	Emma	Emily	Mia
Colorado	Emma	Sophia	Olivia	Isabella	Ava
Connecticut	Emma	Olivia	Isabella	Sophia	Ava
Delaware	Sophia	Emma	Isabella	Ava	Olivia
Dist. of Columbia	Sophia	Emma	Olivia	Charlotte	Genesis
Florida	Isabella	Sophia	Emma	Olivia	Mia
Georgia	Emma	Ava	Isabella	Madison	Olivia
Hawaii	Sophia	Emma	Isabella	Ava	Mia
Idaho	Olivia	Sophia	Emma	Ava	Elizabeth
Illinois	Sophia	Olivia	Isabella	Emma	Ava
Indiana	Emma	Sophia	Olivia	Ava	Isabella
Iowa	Emma	Sophia	Olivia	Harper	Ava
Kansas	Emma	Sophia	Olivia	Isabella	Ava
Kentucky	Emma	Isabella	Sophia	Ava	Abigail
Louisiana	Emma	Ava	Isabella	Olivia	Chloe
Maine	Emma	Sophia	Abigail	Ava	Olivia
Maryland	Sophia	Emma	Ava	Olivia	Isabella
Massachusetts	Emma	Sophia	Olivia	Isabella	Ava
Michigan	Emma	Sophia	Ava	Olivia	Isabella
Minnesota	Emma	Olivia	Sophia	Ava	Avery
Mississippi	Emma	Madison	Ava	Olivia	Chloe
Missouri	Emma	Sophia	Olivia	Ava	Isabella
Montana	Emma	Olivia	Ava	Harper	Sophia
Nebraska	Emma	Olivia	Sophia	Harper	Ava

Baby Names 2014

Nevada	Sophia	Isabella	Emma	Olivia	Mia
New Hampshire	Emma	Sophia	Olivia	Isabella	Ava
New Jersey	Sophia	Isabella	Emma	Olivia	Ava
New Mexico	Sophia	Isabella	Emma	Mia	Aaliyah
New York	Sophia	Isabella	Emma	Olivia	Ava
North Carolina	Emma	Sophia	Ava	Olivia	Isabella
North Dakota	Emma	Olivia	Sophia	Harper	Ava
Ohio	Sophia	Emma	Ava	Olivia	Isabella
Oklahoma	Emma	Sophia	Isabella	Olivia	Abigail
Oregon	Sophia	Emma	Olivia	Isabella	Abigail
Pennsylvania	Emma	Sophia	Ava	Olivia	Isabella
Rhode Island	Sophia	Ava	Emma	Isabella	Olivia
South Carolina	Emma	Madison	Olivia	Isabella	Ava
South Dakota	Emma	Harper	Sophia	Olivia	Ava
Tennessee	Emma	Olivia	Ava	Isabella	Sophia
Texas	Sophia	Isabella	Emma	Mia	Emily
Utah	Emma	Olivia	Sophia	Ava	Lily
Vermont	Ava	Olivia	Emma	Sophia	Ella
Virginia	Sophia	Emma	Olivia	Abigail	Isabella
Washington	Sophia	Emma	Olivia	Isabella	Ava
West Virginia	Emma	Sophia	Isabella	Ava	Olivia
Wisconsin	Emma	Sophia	Olivia	Ava	Isabella
Wyoming	Emma	Sophia	Madison	Elizabeth	Olivia

Top five boys' names by state

State	Rank 1	Rank 2	Rank 3	Rank 4	Rank 5
Alabama	William	James	Mason	John	Jacob
Alaska	James	Ethan	Liam	Gabriel	Jacob
Arizona	Jacob	Liam	Daniel	Ethan	Anthony
Arkansas	William	Mason	James	Jacob	Elijah
California	Jacob	Jayden	Daniel	Ethan	Matthew
Colorado	Liam	Alexander	Jacob	William	Noah
Connecticut	Mason	Jacob	Michael	Liam	Ethan
Delaware	Michael	Anthony	Mason	Liam	Alexander
Dist. of Columbia	William	Alexander	Henry	John	James
Florida	Jayden	Jacob	Ethan	Michael	Mason
Georgia	William	Mason	Jacob	Michael	Jayden
Hawaii	Ethan	Noah	Mason	Elijah	Logan
Idaho	Liam	William	Mason	Samuel	Logan
Illinois	Jacob	Alexander	Noah	Michael	Ethan
Indiana	Liam	Mason	Elijah	Noah	Jacob
Iowa	Liam	Mason	Carter	William	Owen
Kansas	Mason	Liam	William	Noah	Jackson
Kentucky	William	Mason	James	Jacob	Noah
Louisiana	Mason	Jayden	William	Noah	Liam
Maine	Mason	Liam	Noah	Owen	Jacob
Maryland	Mason	Michael	Jacob	Noah	Ethan
Massachusetts	Benjamin	Mason	Ryan	William	Jacob
Michigan	Mason	Liam	Noah	Jacob	Carter
Minnesota	Mason	William	Ethan	Liam	Henry
Mississippi	William	Mason	John	James	Jayden
Missouri	Mason	William	Liam	Jackson	Jacob
Montana	Liam	William	Wyatt	Mason	James
Nebraska	Liam	William	Mason	Jackson	Owen

Baby Names 2014

Nevada	Alexander	Anthony	Daniel	Jayden	Jacob
New Hampshire	Mason	Jackson	Jacob	Liam	Noah
New Jersey	Michael	Anthony	Joseph	Jayden	Matthew
New Mexico	Noah	Jacob	Elijah	Jayden	Daniel
New York	Michael	Jacob	Jayden	Ethan	Mason
North Carolina	William	Mason	Jacob	Elijah	Noah
North Dakota	Liam	Mason	Ethan	James	Noah
Ohio	Mason	Liam	William	Noah	Michael
Oklahoma	Elijah	Noah	Mason	Jacob	Aiden
Oregon	Liam	Mason	Alexander	William	Henry
Pennsylvania	Mason	Liam	Jacob	Michael	Noah
Rhode Island	Mason	Michael	Jacob	Ethan	Noah
South Carolina	William	Mason	James	Elijah	Jayden
South Dakota	Liam	Mason	Jacob	Owen	William
Tennessee	William	Mason	Elijah	James	Jacob
Texas	Jacob	Jayden	Ethan	Noah	Daniel
Utah	William	Liam	Mason	Ethan	Jacob
Vermont	Mason	Noah	Liam	Owen	Logan
Virginia	William	Mason	Liam	Jacob	Elijah
Washington	Mason	Liam	Ethan	Alexander	Benjamin
West Virginia	Mason	Liam	Bentley	Jacob	Hunter
Wisconsin	Mason	Liam	Jackson	Ethan	Owen
Wyoming	Liam	Mason	Logan	William	Wyatt

An Icelandic girl won a 15-year battle in 2013 to keep her birth name after authorities originally deemed "Blaer" too masculine for a girl. As of now she is free to use her real name, which means "light breeze," on her passport and at school.

2

What does 2014 hold for baby names?

Will these trends continue?

Looking forward to 2014, we predict the trend for choosing either old-fashioned or unique names will continue. The Top 10 names will probably go largely unchanged for both boys and girls, but we may become even more varied in the names we give our children, and not just stick to the same safe names. There may also be a backlash against very popular names, as parents opt not to give their child the same name as four or five of their potential school friends.

As parents grow more globally aware and the demographics of North America change, we may see more culturally and ethnically diverse names appearing in these lists, such as Cosette and Zeik. Also, the 100-year rule doesn't seem to be failing, and names that were in the 1914 Top 100 will likely appear in 2014 as well.

Top 10 names from 1914

Boys		Girls	
1.	John	1.	Mary
2.	William	2.	Helen
3.	James	3.	Dorothy
4.	Robert	4.	Margaret
5.	Joseph	5.	Ruth
6.	George	6.	Anna
7.	Charles	7.	Mildred
8.	Edward	8.	Elizabeth
9.	Frank	9.	Frances
10.	Walter	10.	Marie

For girls' names, it's certain that those ending in -a will continue to dominate the Top 20 for at least a while longer. There are currently eight names in that group that end in -a, constituting almost half, and of those eight, three moved up places from the year before (Emma, Mia, and Sofia), four stayed put (Sophia, Olivia, Ava, and Ella), and only one moved down (Isabella). Other similar-sounding names in the Top 20 included Emily, Chloe, Avery, Aubrey, Lily, Natalie, and Zoey, which presumably means that names ending in -y or -ie sounds will also stick around for a few more years. In fact, there are only five names that don't fit into the -a or -y/ie mold—Abigail, Madison, Elizabeth, Addison, and Charlotte—and all of those have also grown considerably in popularity over the last 10 years.

With boys' names, trends are a little harder to predict. There are definitely names which sound very similar in the Top 20, such as Mason, Ethan, William, Liam, Jayden, Aiden, and Benjamin, but there are only a few -ah/-er names sprinkled throughout the Top 20 at the moment, accounting for just four of the entries (Noah, Alexander, Elijah, and Joshua). There's also only a single -y/-ie name in the whole bunch: Anthony. There is a great deal more shuffling in the ranks going on in the boys' names list, with huge differences over the last 10 years—especially in names listed outside the Top 10. Therefore, it's probable that parents expecting baby boys in 2014 will be following trends like nicknames, short names, and religious names instead.

In general, American parents prefer to give their children full-length names rather than shortened versions or nicknames, and this trend doesn't show much sign of stopping. Elizabeth (10th) appears higher up the charts than Ellie (84th), and Robert (61st) is much higher than Bobby (715th). We see this over and over again: Jacob (ranked first) is more popular than Jake (153rd), Abigail (seventh) is higher up than Abby (308th) or Abbie (790th), and Eve (558th) is much further down the charts than Evelyn (27th).

However, it must be said that in some cases picking short versions of traditional names is on the rise. The name Lily (16th last year), for example, is a shortened version of Lillian (25th), while Max (105th) is a shortened version of either Maxwell (116th) or Maximilian (464th); both of these shorter names are clearly more popular than the longer ones. In Europe this is particularly fashionable right now, so perhaps in 2014 we will see much more of this trend, and even a few surprises.

Predicted 2014 Top 10 baby names

Boys	Girls
1. Jacob	1. Sophia
2. Mason	2. Olivia
3. Noah	3. Emma
4. Ethan	4. Isabella
5. William	5. Ava
6. Liam	6. Emily
7. Aiden	7. Mia
8. Alexander	8. Abigail
9. Michael	9. Chloe
10. Jayden	10. Madison

2014 events

Other influences on the names parents choose in 2014 may come from the worlds of sport, politics, and celebrity.

In 2014 there are a couple of major sporting events, and athletes who perform well at them will no doubt become inspirational for new parents. The Winter

What does 2014 hold for baby names?

Olympics and Paralympics, hosted in Sochi, Russia, and the Commonwealth Games, hosted in Glasgow, Scotland, will be capitalizing on the success of the 2012 London Olympics and Paralympics.

The 2012 Olympics and Paralympics proved how inspirational great sporting stars could be. It stands to reason that the heroes of great games inspire some parents to name their children after them, and we were not disappointed during this global event. In fact, there is a chance that the names sporting stars choose for their own children might prove influential, and it wouldn't be the first time: after it was discovered that beach volleyball legend Kerri Walsh-Jennings was pregnant during her most recent gold medal-winning run in London, there was much interest in what she would name her baby. It turned out to be Scout Margery, after the character in *To Kill A Mockingbird*, and 137 sets of parents immediately followed Walsh-Jennings's lead and chose that name for their new daughters.

There is a history of successful athletes creating baby name trends: Jackie Robinson, the first African-American baseball player to play professionally and one of the great legends of the sport, increased the popularity of both the name Jack (for boys) and Jackie (for girls) during the peak of his fame in the US. He can be credited, in large part, for the continuous popularity of these names even in the 21st century—particularly after the film based on his life, *42: The True Story of an American Legend*, came out in 2013 and brought new attention to his story.

Banned names around the world

@—China
Akuma (meaning "devil")—Japan
Anus—Denmark
Chow Tow (meaning "smelly head")—Malaysia
Dalmata (meaning "Dalmatian")—Italy
Gesher (meaning "bridge")—Norway
Monkey—Denmark
Ovnis (meaning "UFO")—Portugal
Q—Sweden
Sor Chai (meaning "insane")—Malaysia
Stompy—Germany

2014 is predicted to be a fairly quiet year in terms of politics, which will make a nice change. Politicians have a hazy history of influencing baby names—it's not true to say that children are frequently named after presidents or prime ministers, but there are exceptions. President Barack Obama's name has yet to enter the Top 1,000 in the US, but Vice President Joe Biden has seen his name increase in popularity during his time in office: the name Joseph has popped back up to position 20 after a spell further down the charts, and looks set for a good comeback. However, unsuccessful presidential candidate Mitt Romney has yet to see his name gain traction—only eight baby boys were given the name Mitt last year.

When Pope Francis I was elected last year, there was a flurry of parents choosing to honor him. The name

Francis has now become a very popular choice for baby boys (and Frances for baby girls) in Catholic communities.

When former British Prime Minister Margaret Thatcher died in 2013, there was speculation that such an iconic figure would influence baby name trends. Looking back, the name Margaret was at the height of its popularity during Thatcher's time as leader, but since the 1980s it hasn't appeared in the Top 100 anywhere and last year it was down to position 178. It doesn't seem to have been affected by her passing, either, as it's been around the same position for nearly 15 years.

Interestingly, it's more popular to name babies after the *children* of politicians, rather than the politicians themselves—Barack Obama's daughters are named Malia and Sasha, and variations of both of these appear in the US's Top 100 names for girls. When British Prime Minister David Cameron's newborn daughter was named Florence in 2010, the UK media went wild, and parents started choosing this name for their baby girls shortly after. In fact, it jumped an astonishing 26 places the year she was born, 11 in the last year, and has moved up 123 overall in the last 10 years. Even Florrie, which is a popular nickname for Florence, now has 27 little girls with the same name in the UK.

Sometimes the phenomenon of naming babies after the children of politicians doesn't even have to mean the successful ones: Sarah Palin's attempt to become Vice President in 2008 fixed the world's eyes upon her, and led to her five children becoming somewhat famous in their own right. Her daughter Bristol, who competed in the 11th season of *Dancing with the Stars* in 2010, saw her name enter the Top 1,000 for the first time in 2009, and last year it was already in the Top 500. Piper, Palin's fourth child, has seen her name steadily increase in popularity since the family came to the nation's attention in 2007, and last year it was in the Top 100—a first for the name.

Significant dates in 2014

Significant anniversaries can potentially influence baby names. In 2014 this includes the 450th anniversary of William Shakespeare's birth, 350 years since New Jersey became a state, 150 years since the birth of composer Richard Strauss, and the 175th birthday of Post-Impressionist artist Paul Cézanne. It will also mark the centenary of the onset of World War I, when President Woodrow Wilson held office.

In popular culture, it will be 50 years since The Beatles were first introduced to the US, and 30 years since the first Apple Macintosh computer went on sale.

Everybody do the dinosaur? Tahra Dactyl, who made headlines for her name after being featured in a local newspaper article last year, must have parents with a sense of humor . . . or a serious interest in paleontology.

In sporting history, 2014 will be 90 years since the first Winter Olympics were held in Chamonix, France; and the 60th anniversary of Roger Bannister running the four-minute mile.

Don't be surprised, therefore, if names linked to these anniversaries start becoming popular. As the media at large begins to broadcast these significant dates, names such as William (Shakespeare), Jersey, Woodrow (Wilson), Richard (Strauss and "Ringo" Starr), Paul (Cézanne and McCartney), John (Lennon), George (Harrison), Apple (yes, really—think Gwyneth Paltrow's daughter), Chamonix, and Roger (Bannister) will start to be considered by parents as potential options for their baby names. And, the more heavily they're promoted, the more frequently they'll be used.

2014 anniversary names

Boys	Girls
Benjamin	Apple
George	Chamonix
John	Frances
Paul	Georgina
Richard (Ringo)	Jersey
Roger	Paula
William	Ricki
Woodrow	Willa

The influence of the entertainment industry

As always, pop culture will probably be the most prominent influence on baby names in the coming year. Celebrities expecting new arrivals from the celebrity stork include *Glee*'s Heather Morris, Halle Berry, Fergie, and Maya Rudolph. If the choices of names these celebrities make are particularly noteworthy, they may well influence the choices made by the general population.

Beyoncé and Jay-Z have applied to trademark their daughter's name, not once but twice. In 2013 the couple asked for "Blue Ivy Carter" to be trademarked exclusively to them, for use with baby products and music.

The Huffington Post released an article recently that broke down the names chosen by celebrities into common categories. Of the 50+ names they analyzed, every single one fell into one of 10 fields: authors (e.g., Harper, David Beckham's daughter), cities (Tennessee, Reese Witherspoon's son), colors (Blue Ivy, Beyoncé's daughter), comic book characters (Kal-El, Nicolas Cage's son), countries (Moroccan, Mariah Carey's son), fruits (Clementine, Ethan Hawke's daughter), New York boroughs (Bronx, Ashlee Simpson's son), music icons (Louis, Sandra Bullock's son), old Hollywood (Ava, Jeremy Renner's daughter), and Shakespearean characters (Exton, Robert Downey Jr.'s son). It's quite impressive that *all* the celebrity names they analyzed slotted so neatly into these 10 categories!

Expected new arrivals in 2013

Evan Rachel Wood and Jamie Bell (Summer 2013)

Michael Bublé and Luisana Lopilato (Summer 2013—boy)

Penélope Cruz and Javier Bardem (Summer 2013)

Maya Rudolph and Paul Thomas Anderson (Summer 2013)

Sarah Burton and David Burton (Summer 2013)

Alec Baldwin and Hilaria Thomas (Summer 2013)

Anna Chlumsky and Shaun So (Summer 2013)

Fergie and Josh Duhamel (Summer 2013)

Mario Lopez and Courtney Laine Mazza (Summer 2013)

Heather Morris and Taylor Hubbell (Summer 2013)

Halle Berry and Olivier Martinez (Fall 2013)

Jenna Wolfe and Stephanie Gosk (Fall 2013)

Jennifer Love Hewitt and Brian Hallisay (Fall 2013)

Kate Winslet and Ned Rocknroll (Fall 2013)

Rachael Leigh Cook and Daniel Gillies (Fall 2013)

Donald Faison and Cacee Cobb (Fall 2013)

What's exciting about pop culture is how everything, from films and TV to books and blogs, can shape the world of baby names.

The year 2014 looks set to be the second year in a row of remakes, reboots, and sequels. Upcoming movies in 2014 include yet another *Wizard of Oz* movie, an animation starring Lea Michele called *Legends of Oz: Dorothy's Return*; *Dumb and Dumber To* with Jim Carrey and Jeff

Baby Names 2014

Daniels; *The Muppets . . . Again!*, with, amongst others, Ricky Gervais and Tina Fey; and remakes of *Jumanji*, *RoboCop*, and *Godzilla*. Some new twists on old concepts include *Maleficent* (*Sleeping Beauty* re-told), starring Angelina Jolie and Elle Fanning; and a new *Popeye* film. There will also be several films based on books, including *The Book Thief*, written originally by Markus Zusak.

When re-makes of old films are released, it's a great chance to analyze baby names over a period of time. You can look back at when the original versions were released and see how trends were affected at the time. For example, when Walt Disney Studios released the original *Sleeping Beauty* cartoon in 1959, the name Aurora immediately moved up 80 places in the charts. Last year it appeared in the Top 200 for the first time, and after the new version, *Maleficent*, comes out in 2014, it may climb higher still.

Another name to watch will be Liesel, which is the main character's name in *The Book Thief*. Liesel/Liesl became extremely popular in 1965 after the film release of Rodgers and Hammerstein's *The Sound of Music*, as it's the name of the Von Trapp family's eldest daughter, and it's possible that a successful version of *The Book Thief* will have a similar impact next year.

If you need inspiration, why not try following the latest trend and consider a character from your favorite book or film? The names Edward, Isabella, and Jacob have all leapt in popularity since the release of *Twilight* by Stephenie Meyer, and Jacob continues to top the charts for baby boys. Even surnames of these characters have increased in popularity: the name Cullen jumped 300 places in a single year.

Popular TV programs set to air in 2014 include a second season of FOX's massive hit *The Following*, a second series of *Nashville*, another season of *Scandal*, and further series of *Glee*, *Community*, *The Good Wife*, *2 Broke Girls*, *Modern Family*, *Grimm*, *The Mindy Project*, *New Girl*, and *Parks and Recreation*. As you may well be heavily pregnant, putting your feet up and watching some TV, you may be influenced by some of these shows. What about Ryan (Hardy; *The Following*), Rayna (Jaymes; *Nashville*), Artie (Abrams; *Glee*), Abed (Nadir; *Community*), Alicia (Florrick; *The Good Wife*), Max (Black; *2 Broke Girls*), Cameron (Tucker; *Modern Family*), Juliette (Silverton; *Grimm*), Mindy (Lahiri; *The Mindy Project*), Cece (*New Girl*), or Leslie (Knope; *Parks and Recreation*)?

2014 rising stars

Boys	Girls
Abed	Alicia
Artie	Aurora
Cameron	Cece
Jeff (Jeffrey)	Dorothy
Jim (James)	Juliette
Markus	Leslie
Max	Liesel
Oz	Mindy
Ricky	Rayna
Ryan	Tina

Reality series will continue to influence our decisions—
especially now that Kim Kardashian has named her daughter
North (also known as Nori, which is a lot cuter), with singer/
rapper Kanye West. The name North probably won't
trend much this year, but Nori could definitely see a rise
in popularity as it's less obscure—although it's a shame it
doesn't start with a "K"! Sister Kourtney's children are Mason
Dash and Penelope Scotland, and even the SSA has admitted
that the astonishing rise of the name Mason can be attributed
to her, saying last year, "Some may attribute this year's rise
to number two to reality TV star Kourtney Kardashian's son."
It's quite impressive that a single baby can have that much
impact on the baby-naming world, but then we are talking
about the Kardashians . . .

3

How to choose a name

Top tips on choosing a name

- **Fall in love with the name(s) you've chosen.** If you plough through this book and none of them jump off the page at you, then you probably haven't found the right one yet. Pick a name that makes you smile because, if you love it, hopefully your child will too.

- **Don't listen to other people.** Sometimes, grandparents and friends will offer baby-naming "advice" to you, which may not always be welcome. If you've got your heart set on a name, keep it a secret until after the birth. Trust your own instincts and remember: no one will really care once they see your baby. Its name will simply be its name.

- **Find a name with meaning.** Having a name that has a back story helps your child understand their significance in the world, so whether you name them after a religious saint or prophet, an important political figure, or a hero in a Greek tragedy, ensure they know where their name came from. They may just be inspired to be as great as their namesake.

- **Have fun.** Picking out names should be fun. Laughing at the ones you'd never dream of choosing can really help you narrow it down to the ones you would. You can also experiment with different spellings, pronunciations, or variations of names you like, or go to places where you might feel inspired.

- **Expand your mind.** Don't rule out the weird ones just yet! As a teenager I went to school with a girl named Siam. Her parents had conceived her on a honeymoon trip to Thailand and gave her the country's old name as a result. She loved growing up and having an unusual name, as I'm sure Egypt (Alicia Keys and Swizz Beatz's son) and Camden John (Nick Lachey and Vanessa Lachey's son) do too. Also, don't be afraid to play around with spellings and pronunciations, even if the results are a little less than conformist. The name Madison, for example, could be spelt Maddison, Madyson, Maddiesun, although you might want to be careful you don't saddle your child with a name that's impossible to spell, pronounce, *and* fit onto a passport application form.

The shortest baby names are only two letters long (Al, Ed, Jo, and Ty), but the longest could be any length imaginable. Popular 11 letter-long names include Bartholomew, Christopher, Constantine, and Maximillian.

- **Try it out.** While you're pregnant, talk to your baby and address it using a variety of your favorite names to see if it responds. There are numerous stories of names being chosen because the baby kicked when it was called Charlie or Aisha, but was suspiciously silent when it was called Dexter or Mildred, so see if it has a preference! Try writing names down and sticking them to your fridge, practicing a few signatures, or saying one out loud enough times to see if you ever get sick of it.

- **Do NOT pick the name of an ex.** No matter how lovely Brad Pitt thought the name "Jennifer" was, it's unlikely Angelina Jolie would have allowed him to use it for one of their daughters. The same is probably true of picking the names of your friends' exes. They are unlikely to thank you if they have to say a name they loathe repeatedly. Just steer clear of any names you know will have problems for other people, paying particular attention to your partner and loved ones.

- **What if you can't agree?** This is probably the trickiest problem in the baby-naming process to solve. It's wise to research a number of names you and your partner are both interested in and make a point of discussing your reasons for liking or disliking them long before the baby is due to be born. The labor and delivery room is probably not the best place to argue as you'll both be tired, emotional, and at least one of you will be in pain. Avoid sticking to your guns on a name one of you really isn't happy with because it might lead to resentment down the line, with your baby caught in the middle. You could try compromising and picking two middle names so you both have a name in there you love, or you could each have five names you're allowed to "veto" but no more. Whichever way you go about it, it is important that you both eventually agree on the name you are giving your baby, even if it means losing out on the one you've had your heart set on for a while.

- **Apps.** With all the new technology literally at our fingertips, how about putting some of it to good use? There are hundreds of new apps for smartphones and tablets that promise to help you narrow down the endless lists of potential names to the one you'll love.

App-arently fake

A word of caution: in 2013, a hoax baby-naming contest went viral because of an app. Belly Ballot, a baby names website and app, claimed it was offering a mother in Los Angeles $5,000 for the right to name her baby. Complete strangers could nominate any name on the app and the one with the most votes would win. After a lot of negative publicity, however, it turned out it was all a publicity stunt, and the woman involved was really an actress.

Popular names from the past

Boys	Girls
Abraham	Agatha
Arthur	Bertha
Edmund	Clara
Emmett	Edith
Franklin	Gladys
Gilbert	Mabel
Jasper	Pearl
Neville	Theodora
Percival	Wilhelmina
Vincent	Winifred

Think to the future

"Always end the name of your child with a vowel, so that when you yell the name will carry.**"**

Bill Cosby

One important aspect of naming your child is thinking ahead to their future. Will the name you've chosen stand the test of time? Will names popular in 2014 remain popular in 2040? Will they be able to confidently enter a room and give a crucial business presentation with an awkward or unpronounceable name? Will they be able to hand their business card over to a potential client without that client looking bemused every time? Even on a smaller scale, can they survive the potential minefields of elementary school and junior high with a name that could easily be shortened to something embarrassing?

Would you want to try catching criminals as Sheriff Apple Blossom or have other politicians take you seriously with a name like Senator Fortune Scarlett? You don't want to give your child a name that they just cannot live with for the rest of their lives, so make your choice based on what's appropriate for an adult as well as a child. To make this easier you might want to choose a longer name that can be shortened or extended as your child desires.

Singer/actor Matt Willis dealt with this very problem in November 2011, when he announced the birth of his new baby son on Twitter. Willis wrote: "I have a son and his name is Ace!" When a follower made a crack about the name, asking if the middle name would be "Ventura," after the popular Jim Carrey character, Willis responded with: "Nearly! Went for Billy so if he wants to be like a f**king banker or something he can use that instead!"

Names that should be banned, but aren't

Anna Banana Baptista

Benson and Hedges (twins)

Ford Mustang

Hairy Berry

Kaos

Laxative Thomas

Masport and Mower (twins)
Midnight Chardonnay
Number 16 Bus Shelter
Spiral Cicada
Superman (changed from 4Real)
Violence

If your child doesn't like the name you've given them because their first and last names make a funny combination, they may choose to use just their first name professionally as an adult. A colleague of mine goes by "Shiney" only—omitting her last name on business cards and emails because it's a euphemism for male genitalia.

French law prohibits all names other than those on an approved list. However, in 2012 French courts allowed one couple to call their child "Daemon" after a vampire character in the TV show *The Vampire Diaries* called Damon—the first such deviation from the approved list in a decade.

Stereotypes—true or false?

Will the name you choose actually affect your child's life? Will names that seem clever make your child brainier? Will names with positive meanings make your child into a happier person? The answer is . . . possibly.

Some experts believe that parents who choose inspirational names for their offspring (Destiny, Serenity, Unique) or names of products they would like to own (Armani, Jaguar, Mercedes) are projecting a future onto their child for them to aspire to, and therefore help shape their child's life. However, there's absolutely no evidence that this actually works!

Inspirational names

Destiny	Joy
Happy	Peace
Heaven	Serenity
Hope	Unique
Innocence	Unity

Aspirational names

Armani	Ferrari
Aston	Jaguar
Bugatti	Mercedes
Chanel	Porsche
Dolce	Prada

One thing you should consider is how your child's name will be perceived by the outside world. Typically, judgments are passed on a person before they are met, and made purely based on their name, such as at job interviews or in school. A survey of 3,000 teachers found that 49% of them make assumptions about their pupils based on their name alone. One in three admitted that certain names spell a troublemaker to them, including Callum, Brandon, Chelsea, and Aleisha, while the names Christopher, Edward, Rebecca, and Charlotte were assumed to belong to brighter children.

The research also indicated that there are certain names more likely to initiate strong responses in people than others. A study analyzed the number of stickers given to children as rewards for good behavior. Children named Abigail and Jacob are more likely to be praised for being well behaved than children named Beth and Josh, and children who do not shorten their name or go by nicknames are more likely to be better behaved, too. However, personality and character have a far greater influence than name alone and, after a while, a name becomes just a name.

Actor Jeremy Sisto took over a month to name his newborn son in 2012, eventually settling on the dubious "Bastian Kick." He claims he and his wife "didn't want to rush into anything."

Ivy League names

Alcott	Graydon
Arthur	Katherine
Beatrice	Martha
Caroline	Robert
Charles	Victoria

Names that sound "clever"

Abner	Shanahan
Cassidy	Todd
Haley	Ulysses
Penelope	Washington
Portia	Wylie

Quirky names

There are lots of advantages to having a quirky name. For one thing, your child's name will never be forgotten by other people, and if they do something influential with their life their name could become an inspiration for other parents. On the other hand, a quirky name often requires a quirky personality. If you don't think your genes could stand up to a name like Satchel or Kerensa, perhaps it's time to think of one a little more run-of-the-mill.

A quirky name often says more about the parents than the child, and their own personalities may affect the personality of their child in a significant way. A conventional family that names their baby John will probably find he becomes a conventional child, whereas a quirky family that names their baby Zanzibar will also find he develops a quirky personality. The name itself is not the leading factor; it's the quirky or conventional behavior encouraged by the parents who chose the name that's important.

Children who are told they have inherited an ancestor's name or are named after an influential character from history seem to be more driven and focused than children who are told disappointingly, "We just liked the sound of it." As a parent, therefore, it seems it's okay to pick an unusual name if you have a story or reason behind it. So naming your child Atticus (after Atticus Finch from Harper Lee's *To Kill A Mockingbird*, known for being a strong and moral character), or even Harper (like the Beckhams did recently), may not be a bad idea . . .

However, be warned: there is also new research from baby website Bounty which says that as many as one in five parents regrets their choice of baby name. Of the 3,000 parents interviewed, 20% said they no longer thought the unusual choice of spelling or pronunciation was appropriate. Around 8% said they were tired of people mispronouncing their child's name, and 10% thought the novelty of the original pick had worn off. They also said they would now pick a new name which had not occurred to them or been an option before.

What not to call your child . . .

In Pennsylvania a few years ago there was a case of a supermarket bakery refusing to ice the words "Happy Birthday, Adolf Hitler" onto a three-year-old's birthday cake. The parents were able to eventually fulfill the order at another shop, but as a result of the publicity surrounding the event, CPS were called in to assess the child's home. Adolf and his siblings JoyceLynn Aryan Nation, and Honszlynn Hinler Jeannie were taken into care.

Controversial names adopted by real people

Adolf Hitler

Beelzebub

Desdemona

Hannibal Lecter

Himmler

Jezebel

Lucifer

Mussolini

Stalin

Voldemort

While avoiding any kind of possible connection to a fictional character is nigh on impossible, you can help make things easier for your child by educating them about their namesake and encouraging them to read more about them. Stay up to date with new cartoons and children's characters in 2014 to prepare both yourself and your child for preschool and childhood. That way they can be proud of their name and have ammunition if things get rough in the schoolyard.

Cartoon characters named after real people

Yogi Bear (named after baseball player Yogi Berra)

Buzz Lightyear (named after astronaut Buzz Aldrin)

Alvin, Simon, and Theodore Chipmunk (named after
  record executives)
Garfield (named after creator Jim Davis's grandfather)
Calvin and Hobbes (named after John Calvin
  [theologian] and Thomas Hobbes [philosopher])
Rock Lee (from *Naruto*, named after Bruce Lee)
Jimmy Neutron (named after the scientist James
  Chadwick, whose nickname was Jimmy Neutron)
Oscar (from *Cerebus*, named after writer Oscar
  Wilde)
Homer, Marge, Lisa, and Maggie Simpson (named
  after creator Matt Groening's family members)
Teenage Mutant Ninja Turtles (all named
  after Renaissance painters: Raphael,
  Michelangelo, Donatello, and Leonardo)

Masculine vs. feminine

How do we define what makes a name masculine or
feminine? Well, it may be to do with the sounds the letters
create, either when written down or spoken aloud. Harder-
sounding combinations (-ter, -it, -ld) tend to be found
in masculine names, and softer-sounding combinations
(-ie, -ay, -la) are more associated with feminine names.
You therefore end up with Sophia, Joanie, and Bella, and
Harold, Walter, David, and Oscar.

If you're planning on choosing a feminine-sounding name,
approach with caution: recent research suggests that girls

who are given particularly "girly" names—think Tiana, Kayla, and Isabella—are much more likely to misbehave when they reach school age. These "feminine" girls were also far less likely to choose subjects at school like math and science, while their sisters with more masculine names—such as Morgan, Alexis, and Ashley—were encouraged to excel in these courses.

Nowadays, names are becoming more androgynous and loads of names appear in both boys' and girls' lists: Madison, Riley, Hayden, and, of course, Alex—some form of which appears in the Top 100 for both boys and girls every year. Therefore, if you want a more gender-neutral name for your new arrival, you won't be alone.

Bizarre baby names from around the country

Boys	Girls
Aero	Ace
Burger	Kaixin
Donathan	Leeloo
Espn	Monalisa
Haven'T	Rogue
Kix	Sesame
Pawk	Thinn
Rysk	Yoga
Zaniel	Zealand

Nicknames

66 Nicknames stick to people, and the most ridiculous are the most adhesive. 99

Thomas C. Haliburton

Nicknames are unavoidable. They can range from the common—Mike from Michael, Sam from Samantha—to the trendy, funny, or downright insulting.

Don't be put off though if the name you love has an unfortunate nickname associated with it—if you don't encourage the use of nicknames, chances are that they won't stick. Another way to avoid embarrassing nicknames is to select one for your child that you actually like so that others don't even get a mention. Call your daughter Elizabeth by the name Liz, Lizzie, or Libby if you don't like Betty or Beth, and no one will even consider the alternatives.

You can pre-empt possible nicknames to some extent by saying the name you've chosen out loud and trying to find rhymes for it. This is a clever way to avoid children's chants and nursery rhyme-type insults, such as Dora the Explorer or Georgie Porgie. But don't be too concerned about playground chants—most children are subjected to them at some point and emerge unscathed.

Pronunciation matters: a Swedish couple were once banned from naming their child "Brfxxccxxmnpccccllllmmnprxvclmncksssqlbb11116," which they claimed was pronounced "Albin."

Your last name

Try to avoid first names that might lead to unfortunate phrases when combined with your last name, to prevent a lifetime of embarrassment for your child. The best way to work out if this might happen is to write down all the names you like alongside your child's last name and have someone else read them out loud. This second pair of eyes and ears might just spot something you didn't.

The age of the internet has given parents a wonderful new weapon in their baby-naming arsenal: the search engine. Before you settle on anything final, try searching for any examples of the complete first, middle, and last name of your new baby. You may find out that your baby has an axe-murderer namesake—or, like one of my colleagues, the same name as a well-known porn star.

Unfortunate first name/last name combinations

Anna Sasin	Isabella Horn
Barb Dwyer	Justin Time
Barry Cade	Mary Christmas
Ben Dover	Oliver Sutton
Duane Pipe	Paige Turner
Grace Land	Russell Sprout
Harry Rump	Stan Still

There is also the danger of your child being subjected to having a Spoonerism made out of their name, where the first letters or syllables get swapped around to form new words. Named after the Reverend Dr William Archibald Spooner (1844–1930), a spoonerism can be created out of almost anything to make clever, amusing, or downright inappropriate phrases instead. An unfortunate and recent example of this would be Angelina Jolie and Brad Pitt's daughter Shiloh, whom they named Shiloh Jolie-Pitt to avoid the inevitable Shiloh Pitt spoonerism.

Twitter has recently become a hot spot for spoonerisms, with celebrities such as Justin Bieber and Nick Jonas calling each other "Bustin Jieber" and "Jick Nonas." Well, no one ever said spoonerisms have to make sense . . .

Famous name spoonerisms

Gene Kelly (keen jelly)

Jude Law (lewd jaw)

Justin Bieber (bustin jieber)

Nick Jonas (jick nonas)

Paul Walker (wall porker)

Sarah Palin (para sailing)

Shiloh Pitt (pile o' s***)

Shirley Bassey (burly chassis)

The website Name of the Year pronounced a Dutch pharmacoepidemiologist as the winner of their annual competition last year: Taco B. M. Monster. He beat Monquarius Mungo, Atticus Disney, and La'Peaches Pitts to win the top spot.

Initials

What last name will your baby have? Will it lend itself easily to amusing acronyms when coupled with certain first and middle names? My brother-in-law was going to be called Andrew Steven Schmitt before he was born, until his parents realized at the last minute what his initials would spell . . .

It's worth taking the time to think about how credit cards display names or seeing your child's name written out on a form. Nobody should have to go through life known as S. Lugg because their parents didn't think that far ahead.

Amusing initials

Al E. Gador	I. C. Blood
Angie O. Graham	I. P. Freely
Earl E. Bird	Kay F. Cee
Gene E. Yuss	S. Lugg
H. I. Vee	Warren T.

Medical terms used as names

The following list was provided by a practicing midwife, who has vivid recollections of parents thinking they were naming their children something unique and original, only to be told the name they'd chosen was a medical term.

Chlamydia (pronounced cler-mid-EE-ya)
Eczema (pronounced ex-SEE-mah)
Female (pronounced fuh-MAH-lee)
Latrine (pronounced lah-TREE-nee)
Meconium (pronounced meh-COH-nee-um)
Syphilis (pronounced see-PHIL-iss)
Testicles (pronounced TESS-tee-clees)
Urine (pronounced yer-REE-nee)
Vagina (pronounced vaj-EE-nah)

Using family names

Some families have a strong tradition of using names for babies that come from the family tree. There are instances where naming your son Augustine VIII is simply not an option; it's a rule. Another way families do this is to give children the name of their parent of the same sex and add "Junior" (Jr.) to the end. This could only create a problem if that child then decides to carry on the tradition and name their child after themselves—after all, who wants to be known as Frederick Jr. Jr.?

There are pros and cons with using family names.

- **Pro:** Your child will feel part of a strong tradition, which will create a sense of security for them and help make them feel a complete member of the family.

- **Pro:** If you're having a problem selecting a name you and your partner both agree on, this is a very simple solution and will make your new child's family very happy.

- **Con:** You might not actually like the name that's being passed down. Naming your child the 12th Thumbelina in a row might not actually hold the same attraction for you as for the generation before.

- **Con:** Another drawback could be if the cultural associations with that name have changed in your lifetime and it is no longer appropriate.

In 2011 Pope Benedict decreed that all names should come from the Christian calendar. Italy promptly forbade one couple from naming their child "Venerdi," meaning "Friday," because it would open the boy up to ridicule and mockery. The parents threatened to name their next son "Mercoledi," meaning "Wednesday," in response.

One way to include a family name is to compromise. You could use the name as a middle name, or refer to your baby by a nickname instead. Another possible solution is to use monikers—if your family is insisting your daughter be called Jade, maybe you could choose Giada instead. Or if your partner is determined the next child be called Michael after himself and it turns out to be a girl, choose Michaela in its place. In many Jewish families the tradition is to take the name of a deceased relative and give it to a new baby. If this thought fills you with dread, you could opt for a possible solution a lot of families adopt, which is to use the first initial instead. If you're not keen on Solomon, pick Samuel; if you don't like Ruth, choose Rebecca.

Spellings and pronunciation

Once you've finally agreed upon a name, it's time to consider how you wish it to be spelt and pronounced. Some parents love experimenting with unusual variations of traditional names, while others prefer for names to be instantly recognizable.

Try to avoid making a common name too long or too unusual in its spelling as this will be the first thing your child learns how to write. They will also have to spell it out constantly during their lifetime, as other people misspell or mispronounce their name. Substituting the odd "i" for a "y" isn't too bad, but turning the name Jonathan into Jonnaythanne doesn't do anyone any favors.

The US has seen an increase in "text speak" spellings

An	Jayk
Camron	Lora
Conna	Patryk
Ema	Samiul
Esta	Summa
Flicity	Wilym

A palindrome name is a name that is spelt the same backwards and forwards, as with Bob, Elle, Eve, and Hannah.

Middle names

Giving your child a middle name is generally acknowledged to be standard practice these days. In fact, it has become fairly uncommon to name a child *without* a middle name, although the use of second and third names only became popular around the turn of the 20th century. Before then, giving a child a middle name was seen as a status symbol; it was only really used when a man married a higher-class woman and they wanted to keep the woman's maiden name as a reminder of that child's heritage. Once the fashion caught on it became very popular to give more than one middle name to children of status, but it's only been since the 1900s that it has become standard for everyone. Regardless of your status, a middle name can have just as much of an impact as a first name, so your choice for your own baby should be made as carefully as the decision about their first name.

Here are some common trends in 2014 to help you choose.

- **Opposite-length names.** It has become very popular to give a child either a long first name and short middle name (e.g., Jennifer Ruth, Nicholas John) or vice versa.

- **Name from the family tree.** Honoring your ancestors is another popular trend for 2014. Parents are frequently looking back to their own lineage for interesting, unusual, or influential names. It is becoming more and more common to give a parent's first name as a middle name to newborns.

- **Unusual names.** Parents who like a quirky name but aren't quite brave enough to give it to their child as a first name are using it as a middle name.

Long, longer, and longest

How about trying to beat the record for world's longest name? The British teenager named Captain Fantastic Faster Than Superman Spiderman Batman Wolverine Hulk And The Flash Combined, changed his name from George Garratt in 2008. At the time, he claimed to have the longest name in the world, replacing Texan woman Rhoshandiatellyneshiaunneveshenk Koyaanisquatsiuth Williams, whose 57-letter name paled in comparison to Captain's 81. However, a woman from the UK beat

both these records in 2012, when she changed her
name by legal deed poll from Dawn McManus to . . .
and get ready for this: Red Wacky League Antlez Broke
the Stereo Neon Tide Bring Back Honesty Coalition
Feedback Hand of Aces Keep Going Captain Let's
Pretend Lost State of Dance Paper Taxis Lunar Road Up
Down Strange All And I Neon Sheep Eve Hornby Faye
Bradley AJ Wilde Michael Rice Dion Watts Matthew
Appleyard John Ashurst Lauren Swales Zoe Angus
Jaspreet Singh Emma Matthews Nicola Brown Leanne
Pickering Victoria Davies Rachel Burnside Gil Parker
Freya Watson Alisha Watts James Pearson Jacob
Sotheran Darley Beth Lowery Jasmine Hewitt Chloe
Gibson Molly Farquhar Lewis Murphy Abbie Coulson
Nick Davies Harvey Parker Kyran Williamson Michael
Anderson Bethany Murray Sophie Hamilton Amy Wilkins
Emma Simpson Liam Wales Jacob Bartram Alex Hooks
Rebecca Miller Caitlin Miller Sean McCloskey Dominic
Parker Abbey Sharpe Elena Larkin Rebecca Simpson
Nick Dixon Abbie Farrelly Liam Grieves Casey Smith
Liam Downing Ben Wignall Elizabeth Hann Danielle
Walker Lauren Glen James Johnson Ben Ervine Kate
Burton James Hudson Daniel Mayes Matthew Kitching
Josh Bennett Evolution Dreams. Red (formerly Dawn)
changed her name to this 161-word whopper to
raise money for her charity, Red Dreams (now her
first and last name), set up after the death of
her son. And yes, she really did it!

You may have already decided what middle name to give your child due to tradition or culture, in which case the following advice may be moot. In Hispanic cultures, for example, middle names are often the mother's surname or other name to promote that matriarchal lineage. Similarly, parents who have not taken each other's surnames or are not married may choose to give their child one surname as a middle name and one as a last name so both parents are represented. Other traditions may use an old family name, passed down to each first-born son or daughter to encourage a sense of family pride and history. A decision about what middle name to pass on may have therefore already been made for you, even before your own birth.

Unique middle names are very much *en vogue* right now with celebrities. The Beckhams chose "Seven" for their daughter's middle name, and there has been much discussion in the media as to why—could it be because Beckham's jersey number was seven, or that the little girl was born during the seventh hour, on the seventh day of the week, during the seventh month? Was it because the number seven is traditionally lucky? Who knows . . .

Sweden has a pretty strict naming law, enacted in 1982, which says: "First names shall not be approved if they can cause offense or can be supposed to cause discomfort for the one using it, or names which for some obvious reason are not suitable as a first name." However, they did recently approve the use of "Google" as a middle name.

Many people actually choose to go by their middle name instead of their forename, so it could be seen as a safety net if you're worried your child won't like their name.

Some famous examples of multiple middle names include Canadian actor Kiefer Sutherland, who has shortened his name considerably from Kiefer William Frederick Dempsey George Rufus Sutherland. Even the British royal family likes to give many middle names: Prince Charles's full name is Charles Philip Arthur George Mountbatten-Windsor, and Prince William is William Arthur Philip Louis Mountbatten-Windsor.

Celebrities who go by middle names

Antonio Banderas (José Antonio Domínguez Banderas)
Ashton Kutcher (Christopher Ashton Kutcher)
Bob Marley (Nesta Robert Marley)
Brad Pitt (William Bradley Pitt)
Brooke Shields (Christa Brooke Camille Shields)
Dakota Fanning (Hannah Dakota Fanning)
Evangeline Lilly (Nicole Evangeline Lilly)
Hugh Laurie (James Hugh Calum Laurie)
Kelsey Grammer (Allen Kelsey Grammer)
Reese Witherspoon (Laura Jeanne Reese
    Witherspoon)
Rihanna (Robyn Rihanna Fenty)
Will Ferrell (John William Ferrell)

Naming twins, triplets, and more

If you have discovered you are expecting multiples, congratulations! Naming multiples needn't be any different to naming a single child . . . unless you want it to be. You could stick to the same process everyone else does, by picking an individual name for each individual child. Even "Octomom" Nadya Suleman chose eight different names for her octuplets, although they do all sound reasonably similar: Isaiah, Jeremiah, Jonah, Josiah, Maliyah, Makai, Nariyah, and Noah.

Twin names with the same meaning

Bernard and Brian (strong)
Daphne and Laura (laurel)
Deborah and Melissa (bee)
Dorcas and Tabitha (gazelle)
Elijah and Joel (God)
Eve and Zoe (life)
Irene and Salome (peace)
Lucius and Uri (light)
Lucy and Helen (light)
Sarah and Almira (princess)

Another option is to go with a theme. Try anagrams or names in reverse, or give each child the same initials or names with the same meaning. You could even do this if you're not expecting multiples, like the Duggar family

of Arkansas, who have given each of their 19 children
the initial "J"—Joshua, Jana, John-David, Jill, Jessa, Jinger,
Joseph, Josiah, Joy-Anna, Jedidiah, Jeremiah, Jason, James,
Justin, Jackson, Johannah, Jennifer, Jordyn-Grace, and Josie.
Their last arrival was named Jubilee, although she sadly
passed away in late 2011. Eldest son Joshua is currently
expecting his third child with wife Anna, and so far their
children all have "M" names.

A Texan woman gave birth to two sets of identical twin
boys on the same day in 2013. Conceived naturally,
the chances of which are one in 70 million, Tressa and
Manuel Montalvo named their miracles Ace, Blaine,
Cash, and Dylan (ABCD).

Mariah Carey and Nick Cannon chose to use names starting
with the same letter when naming their twins. Before
announcing the names, Nick posted a clue to the names on
Twitter, "So we r bout 2 reveal the actual names and b4 we
tell em 2 our friends etc. both begin w/M's!!!!" The couple
then announced the arrival of Monroe and Moroccan Scott,
girl and boy twins. "Scott" is the same middle name as
Nick Cannon and his grandmother's maiden name, and as
Mariah Carey doesn't have a middle name, they skipped
one for Monroe too.

Of course, when all's said and done you can just stick
to giving each child a name unique to them. For triplets,
quads, and more, this is probably an easier choice than
twisting your head around three names with the same
meaning, or trying to create four anagrams you like for all of

your babies. Some parents do like to use a theme though, such as going down the alphabet (think Alastair, Benjamin, Christopher, and David), or doing what the famous acting Phoenix clan did and giving each child a name to do with nature: River, Rain, Joaquin (Leaf), Liberty, and Summer.

Popular twin names

Brandon and Brian

Daniel and David

Ella and Emma

Faith and Hope

Gabriella and Isabella

Isaac and Isaiah

Jacob and Joshua

Madison and Morgan

Matthew and Michael

Taylor and Tyler

Celebrity twin names of the past few years

Adalynn and Noah (Chris and Deanna Daughtry)

Darby and Sullivan (Patrick Dempsey and Jillian Fink)

Eddy and Nelson (Celine Dion and René Angélil)

Eden and Savannah (Marcia Cross and Tom Mahoney)

Gideon and Harper (Neil Patrick Harris and David Burtka)

Hazel and Phinnaeus (Julia Roberts and Danny Moder)

Jesse and Journey (Jenna Jameson and Tito Ortiz)
Max and Bob (Charlie Sheen and Brooke Mueller)
Max and Emme (Jennifer Lopez and Marc Anthony)
Monroe and Moroccan Scott (Mariah Carey and Nick
   Cannon)
Poppy and Charlie (Anna Paquin and Stephen Moyer)
Vivienne Marcheline and Knox Léon
   (Angelina Jolie and Brad Pitt)

Names for triplets

Abel, Bela, and Elba (anagrams)
Aidan, Diana, and Nadia (anagrams)
Amber, Jade, and Ruby (jewels)
Amy, May, and Mya (anagrams)
April, May, and June (months)
Ava, Eva, and Iva (similar)
Daisy, Lily, and Rose (flowers)
Jay, Raven, and Robin (birds)
Leah, Lianne, and Liam (similar)
Olive, Violet, and Sage (colors)
River, Rain, and Summer (nature)

The first quintuplets (and perhaps the most famous, still)
ever known to have survived infancy were the Dionne
family, from Canada. Born in 1934, their names were
Yvonne, Annette, Cécile, Émilie, and Marie.

part two

Boys' Names

 **Boys' names**

Aaron
Hebrew, meaning 'mountain of strength'.

Abasi
Egyptian, meaning 'male'.

Abdiel
Biblical, meaning 'servant of God'.

Abdul
(alt. Abdullah)
Arabic, meaning 'servant of God'. Often followed with a suffix indicating who Abdul is the servant of (e.g. Abdul-Basit, servant of the creator).

Abel
Hebrew, meaning 'breath' or 'breathing spirit'. Associated with the Biblical son of Adam and Eve who was killed by his brother Cain.

Abelard
German, meaning 'resolute'.

Aberforth
Gaelic, meaning 'mouth of the river Forth'. Name of Dumbledore's brother in the Harry Potter series.

Abner
Hebrew, meaning 'father of light'.

Abraham
(alt. Abe)
Hebrew, meaning 'exalted father'.

Absaglom
(alt. Absalon)
Hebrew, meaning 'father/ leader of peace'.

A

Acacio
Greek origin, meaning 'thorny tree'. Now widely used in Spain.

Ace
English, meaning 'number one' or 'the best'.

Achebe
Nigerian, meaning 'may the earth protect us'. Last name of writer Chinua Achebe.

Achilles
Greek, mythological hero of Trojan war, whose heel was his only weak spot.

Achim
Hebrew, meaning 'God will establish'; Polish, meaning 'The Lord exalts'.

Ackerley
Old English, meaning 'oak meadow'. Often used as last name, with many similarly spelt variants.

Adalberto
Germanic/Spanish, meaning 'nobly bright'.

Adam
(alt. Adome, Admon)
Hebrew, meaning 'man' or 'earth'. First man to walk the earth, accompanied by Eve.

Adão
Portuguese variant of Adam, meaning 'earth'.

Addison
Old English, meaning 'son of Adam'. Also used as a female name.

Ade
African, meaning 'peak' or 'pinnacle'.

Adelard
Teutonic, meaning 'brave' or 'noble'.

Adelbert
Old German form of Albert.

Aden
Gaelic, meaning 'fire'.

Adin
Hebrew, meaning 'slender' or 'voluptuous'; Swahili, meaning 'ornamental'.

Aditya
Sanskrit, meaning 'belonging to the sun'.

Adlai
Hebrew, meaning 'God is just', or sometimes 'ornamental'.

Adler
Old German, meaning 'eagle'.

Adley
English, meaning 'son of Adam'.

Adolph
(alt. Adolfo)
Old German, meaning 'noble majestic wolf'. Popularity of the name plummeted after the Second World War, for obvious reasons.

Adonis
Phoenician, meaning 'Lord'.

Adrian
Latin origin, meaning 'from Hadria', a town in northern Italy.

Adriel
Hebrew, meaning 'of God's flock'.

Aeneas
Greek/Latin origin, meaning 'to praise'. Name of the hero who founded Rome in Virgil's *Aeneid*.

Aero
Greek, meaning 'fair'.

Aeson
Greek origin, father of Jason.

Afonso
Portuguese, meaning 'eager noble warrior'.

Agamemnon
Greek, meaning 'leader of the assembly'. Figure in mythology, commanded the Greeks at the siege of Troy.

Agathon
Greek, meaning 'good' or 'superior'.

Agustin
Latin/Spanish, meaning 'venerated'.

Ahab
Hebrew, meaning 'father's brother'. Pleasant way to address an uncle.

Movie inspirations

Anakin (Star Wars)
Edward (Twilight)
Forrest (*Forrest Gump*)
Harry (Harry Potter)
Indiana (*Raiders of the Lost Ark*)
Inigo (*The Princess Bride*)
Korben (*The Fifth Element*)
Marty (*Back to the Future*)
Red (*The Shawshank Redemption*)
Vito (*The Godfather*)

A

Ahijah
Hebrew, meaning 'brother of God' or 'friend of God'.

Ahmed
Arabic/Turkish, meaning 'worthy of praise'.

Aidan
Gaelic, meaning 'little fire'.

Aidric
Old English, meaning 'oaken'.

Airyck
Old Norse, from Eric, meaning 'eternal ruler'.

Ajani
African, meaning 'he fights for what he is'; Sanskrit, meaning 'of noble birth'.

Ajax
Greek, meaning 'mourner of the Earth'. A Greek hero from the siege of Troy.

Ajay
Indian, meaning 'unconquerable'.

Ajit
Indian, meaning 'invincible'.

Akeem
Arabic, meaning 'wise or insightful'.

Akio
Japanese, meaning 'bright man'.

Akira
Japanese, meaning 'intelligent'.

Akiva
Hebrew, meaning 'to protect' or 'to shelter'.

Akon
American, meaning 'flower'.

Aksel
Hebrew/Danish, meaning 'father of peace'.

Aladdin
Arabic, meaning 'servant of Allah'. Character in *The Arabian Nights*, made popular by Disney.

Alan
(alt. Allan, Allen, Allyn, Alun)
Gaelic, meaning 'rock'.

Alaric
Old German, meaning 'noble regal ruler'.

Alastair
(alt. Alasdair, Allister)
Greek/Gaelic, meaning 'defending men'.

Alban
Latin, meaning 'from Alba'; Welsh and Scottish Gaelic word for 'Scotland'.

Alberic
Germanic, meaning 'Elfin king'.

Albert
Old German, meaning 'noble, bright, famous'.

Albus
(alt. Albin)
Latin, meaning 'white'. Also the first name of Albus Dumbledore, headmaster of Hogwarts School in the Harry Potter series.

Alcaeus
Greek, meaning 'strength'.

Alden
Old English, meaning 'old friend'.

Aldis
English, meaning 'from the old house'.

Aldo
Italian origin, meaning 'old' or 'elder'.

Aldric
English, meaning 'old king'.

Alec
(alt. Alek)
English, meaning 'defending men'.

Aled
Welsh, meaning 'child' or 'offspring'.

Aleph
Hebrew, meaning 'first letter of the alphabet', or 'leader'.

Alessio
Italian, meaning 'defender'.

Alexander
(alt. Alex, Alexandro, Alessandro, Alejandro)
Greek, meaning 'defending men'.

Alexei
Russian, meaning 'defender'.

Alfonso
Germanic/Spanish, meaning 'noble and prompt, ready to struggle'.

Alford
Old English, meaning 'old river/ford'.

Alfred
(alt. Alf, Alfi, Alfie, Alfredo)
English, meaning 'elf' or 'magical counsel'. Name of legendary English king Alfred the Great.

Algernon
French, meaning 'with a moustache'.

Ali
(alt. Allie)
Arabic, meaning 'noble, sublime'.

Alijah
Hebrew, meaning 'the Lord is my God'.

Allison
English, meaning 'noble'.

Alois
German, meaning 'famous warrior'.

Alok
Indian, meaning 'cry of triumph'.

Alon
Jewish, meaning 'oak tree'.

Alonso
(alt. Alonzo)
Germanic, meaning 'noble and ready'.

Aloysius
Italian saint's name, meaning 'fame and war'.

Alpha
First letter of the Greek alphabet.

Alphaeus
Hebrew, meaning 'changing'.

Alpin
Gaelic, meaning 'related to the Alps'.

Altair
Arabic, meaning 'flying' or 'bird'.

Alter
Yiddish, meaning 'old man'.

Alton
Old English, meaning 'old town'.

Alva
Latin, meaning 'white'.

Alvie
German, meaning 'army of elves'.

Alvin
English, meaning 'friend of elves'.

Alwyn
(alt. Alwen)
Welsh, meaning 'wise friend'.

Amachi
African, meaning 'who knows what God has brought us through this child'.

Amadeus
Latin, meaning 'God's love'.

Amadi
African, meaning 'appeared destined to die at birth'.

Amado
Spanish, meaning 'God's love'.

Amador
Spanish, meaning 'one who loves'.

Amari
Hebrew, meaning 'given by God'.

Amarion
Arabic, meaning 'populous, flushing'.

Amasa
Hebrew, meaning 'burden'.

Ambrose
Greek, meaning 'undying, immortal'.

Americo
Germanic, meaning 'ever powerful in battle'.

Amias
Latin, meaning 'loved'.

Amir
Hebrew, meaning 'prince' or 'treetop'.

Amit
Hindu, meaning 'friend'.

Ammon
Egyptian, meaning 'the hidden one'.

Amory
German/English, meaning 'work' and 'power'.

Amos
Hebrew, meaning 'encumbered' or 'burdened'.

Anacletus
Latin, meaning 'called back' or 'invoked'.

Anakin
American, meaning 'warrior'. Made famous by Anakin Skywalker in the *Star Wars* films.

Ananias
Greek/Italian, meaning 'answered by the Lord'.

Anastasius
Latin, meaning 'resurrection'.

Anat
Jewish, meaning 'water spring'.

Anatole
Greek, meaning 'cynical but without malice'.

Anders
Greek, meaning 'lion man'.

A

Anderson
English, meaning 'male'.

Andrew
(alt. Andreas, Andre, Andy)
Greek, meaning 'man' or
'warrior'.

Androcles
Greek, meaning 'glory of a
warrior'.

Angel
Greek, meaning 'messenger'.

Angelo
Italian, meaning 'angel'.

Angus
Scottish, meaning 'one choice'.

Anil
Sanskrit, meaning 'air' or
'wind'.

Anselm
German, meaning 'helmet of
God'.

Anson
English, meaning 'son of
Agnes'.

Anthony
(alt. Ant, Antony)
English, from the old Roman
family name. Mark Antony
(Marcus Antonius) was also
Cleopatra's lover.

Antipas
Israeli, meaning 'for all or
against all'.

Antwan
Old English, meaning
'flower'.

Apollo
Greek, meaning 'to destroy'.
Greek god of the sun.

Apostolos
Greek, meaning 'apostle'.

Ara
Armenian, from the legendary
king of the same name.

Aragorn
Literary, used by Tolkien in *The
Lord of the Rings* trilogy.

Aram
Hebrew, meaning 'Royal
Highness'.

Aramis
Latin, meaning 'swordsman'.

Arcadio
Greek/Spanish, meaning
'paradise'.

Archibald
(alt. Archie)
Old German, meaning
'genuine/bold/brave'.

Ardell
Latin, meaning 'eager/burning with enthusiasm'.

Arden
Celtic, meaning 'high'.

Ares
Greek, meaning 'ruin'. Son of Zeus and Greek god of war.

Ari
Hebrew, meaning 'lion' or 'eagle'.

Arias
Germanic, meaning 'lion'.

Ariel
Hebrew, meaning 'lion of God'. One of the archangels, the angel of healing and new beginnings.

Arild
Old Norse, meaning 'battle commander'.

Aris
Greek, meaning 'best figure'.

Ariston
Greek, meaning 'the best'.

Aristotle
Greek, meaning 'best'. Also the philosopher.

Arjun
Sanskrit, meaning 'white'.

Arkady
Greek, region of central Greece.

Arlan
Gaelic, meaning 'pledge' or 'oath'.

Arlie
Old English place name, meaning 'eagle wood'.

Arlis
Hebrew, meaning 'pledge'.

Arlo
Spanish, meaning 'barberry tree'.

Armani
(alt. Armand)
Old German, meaning 'soldier'. Nowadays closely associated with the Italian designer.

Arnaldo
Spanish, meaning 'eagle power'.

Arnav
Indian, meaning 'the sea'.

Arnold
Old German, meaning 'eagle ruler'.

A

Arrow
English, from the common word denoting weaponry.

Art
Irish, from the name of a warrior in Irish mythology, Art Oenfer (Art the Lonely).

Arthur
(alt. Artie, Artis)
Celtic, probably from 'artos', meaning 'bear'. Made famous by the tales of King Arthur and the Knights of the Round Table.

Arturo
Celtic or Italian, meaning 'strong as a bear'.

Arvel
From the Welsh 'Arwel', meaning 'wept over'.

Arvid
English, meaning 'eagle in the woods'.

Arvind
Indian, meaning 'red lotus'.

Arvo
Finnish, meaning 'value' or 'worth'.

Arwen
Welsh, meaning 'fair' or 'fine'.

Asa
Hebrew, meaning 'doctor' or 'healer'.

Asante
African, meaning 'thank you'.

Asher
Hebrew, meaning 'fortunate' or 'lucky'.

Ashley
Old English, meaning 'ash meadow'.

Ashok
Sanskrit, meaning 'not causing sorrow'.

Ashton
English, meaning 'settlement in the ash-tree grove'.

Aslan
Turkish, meaning 'lion'. Strongly associated with the lion from C. S. Lewis's *The Lion, The Witch, and The Wardrobe*.

Asriel
Hebrew, meaning 'help of God'.

Astrophel
Latin, meaning 'star lover'.

Athanasios
Greek, meaning 'eternal life'.

A

Atílio
Portuguese, meaning 'father'.

Atlas
Greek, meaning 'to carry'. In Greek mythology Atlas was a Titan forced to carry the weight of the heavens.

Atlee
Hebrew, meaning 'God is just'.

Atticus
Latin, meaning 'from Athens'.

Auberon
Old German, meaning 'royal bear'.

Aubrey
Old German, meaning 'power'.

Auden
Old English, meaning 'old friend'.

Audie
Old English, meaning 'noble strength'.

August
Latin, meaning 'magnificent'.

Augustas
(alt. Augustus)
Latin, meaning 'venerated'.

Aurelien
French, meaning 'golden'.

Austin
Latin, meaning 'venerated'. Also the Texas city.

Literary names

Atticus (*To Kill A Mockingbird*, Harper Lee)
Cash (*As I Lay Dying*, William Faulkner)
Gatsby (*The Great Gatsby*, F. Scott Fitzgerald)
Holden (*The Catcher in the Rye*, J. D. Salinger)
Ishmael (*Moby Dick*, Herman Melville)
Rhett (*Gone With The Wind*, Margaret Mitchell)
Santiago (*The Old Man and the Sea*, Ernest Hemingway)
Uncas (*The Last of the Mohicans*, James Fenimore Cooper)
Winfield (*The Grapes of Wrath*, John Steinbeck)
Yossarian (*Catch-22*, Joseph Heller)

A

Avi
Hebrew, meaning 'father of a multitude of nations'.

Awnan
Irish, meaning 'little Adam'.

Axel
Hebrew, meaning 'father is peace'. Made famous by Guns 'n' Roses frontman Axl Rose.

Azarel
(alt. Azaryah)
Hebrew, meaning 'helped by God'.

Azriel
Hebrew, meaning 'God is my help'.

Azuko
African, meaning 'past glory'.

B Boys' names

Babe
American, meaning 'baby'.
Associated with baseball legend
'Babe' Ruth.

Baden
German, meaning 'battle'.

Bailey
English, meaning 'bailiff'.

Baird
Scottish, meaning 'poet' or
'one who sings ballads'.

Bakari
Swahili, meaning 'hope' or
'promise'.

Baker
English, from the word 'baker'.

Baldwin
Old French, meaning 'bold,
brave friend'.

Balin
Old English, meaning
'powerful and strong'. Balin
was one of the Knights of the
Round Table.

Balthazar
Babylonian, meaning 'protect
the king'.

Balvinder
Hindu, meaning 'merciful,
compassionate'.

Bannon
Irish, meaning 'descendant of
O'Banain'.

Barack
African, meaning 'blessed'.
Made popular by the 44th
President of the United States
Barack Obama.

B

Barclay
Old English, meaning 'birch tree meadow'.

Barker
Old English, meaning 'shepherd'.

Barnaby
(alt. Barney)
Greek, meaning 'son of consolation'.

Barnard
English, meaning 'strong as a bear'.

Baron
Old English, meaning 'young warrior'.

Barrett
English, meaning 'strong as a bear'.

Barron
Old German, meaning 'old clearing'.

Barry
Irish Gaelic, meaning 'fair haired'.

Bartholomew
(alt. Bart, Barty)
Hebrew, meaning 'son of the farmer'.

Barton
Old English, meaning 'barley settlement'.

Baruch
Hebrew, meaning 'blessed'.

Bascom
Old English, meaning 'from Bascombe'.

Bashir
Arabic, meaning 'well-educated' and 'wise'.

Basil
Greek, meaning 'royal, kingly'.

Basim
Arabic, meaning 'smile'.

Bastien
Greek, meaning 'revered'.

Baxter
Old English, meaning 'baker'.

Bayard
French, meaning 'auburn haired'.

Bayo
Nigerian, meaning 'to find joy'.

Baz
Irish Gaelic, meaning 'fair-haired'.

B

Beau
French, meaning 'handsome'.

Beck
Old Norse, meaning 'stream'.

Beckett
Old English, meaning 'beehive' or 'bee cottage'. Associated with the Irish writer Samuel Beckett.

Beckham
English, meaning 'homestead by the stream'. Made famous by English soccer star David Beckham.

Béla
Hungarian, meaning 'within'.

Biblical names

David
Jesus
John
Joseph
Luke
Mark
Matthew
Michael
Paul
Peter
Simon

Belarius
Shakespearean, meaning 'a banished lord'.

Benedict
Latin, meaning 'blessed'.

Benjamin
(alt. Ben, Benny)
Hebrew, meaning 'son of the south'.

Bennett
French/Latin vernacular form of Benedict, meaning 'blessed'.

Benoit
French form of Benedict, meaning 'blessed'.

Benson
English, meaning 'son of Ben'.

Bentley
Old English, meaning 'bent grass meadow'.

Benton
Old English, meaning 'town in the bent grass'.

Beriah
Hebrew, meaning 'in fellowship' or 'in envy'.

Bernard
(alt. Bernie)
Germanic, meaning 'strong, brave bear'.

B

Berry
Old English, meaning 'berry'.

Bert
(alt. Bertie, Bertram, Bertrand, Berty)
Old English, meaning 'illustrious'.

Berton
Old English, meaning 'bright settlement'.

Bevan
Welsh, meaning 'son of Evan'.

Bicknell
Old English, meaning 'from Bicknell'.

Bilal
Arabic, meaning 'wetting, refreshing'.

Bill
(alt. Billy)
English, from William, meaning 'determined' or 'resolute'.

Birch
Old English, meaning 'bright' or 'shining'.

Birger
Norwegian, meaning 'rescue'.

Bishop
Old English, meaning 'bishop'.

Bjorn
Old Norse, meaning 'bear'.

Bladen
Hebrew, meaning 'hero'.

Blaine
Irish Gaelic, meaning 'yellow'.

Blair
English, meaning 'plain'.

Blaise
French, meaning 'lisp' or 'stutter'.

Blake
Old English, meaning 'dark, black'. William Blake was a highly influential poet, painter and printmaker.

Blas
(alt. Blaze)
German, meaning 'firebrand'.

Bo
Scandinavian, from Robert, meaning 'bright fame'.

Boaz
Hebrew, meaning 'swiftness' or 'strength'.

Bob
(alt. Bobby)
Old German, from Robert, meaning 'bright fame'.

Boden
(alt. Bodie)
Scandinavian, meaning 'shelter'.

Bogumil
Slavic, meaning 'God's favor'.

Bond
Old English, meaning 'peasant farmer'.

Boris
Slavic, meaning 'battle glory'.

Bosten
English, meaning 'town by the woods'.

Bowen
Welsh, meaning 'son of Owen'.

Boyd
Scottish Gaelic, meaning 'yellow'.

Brad
(alt. Bradley)
Old English, meaning 'broad' or 'wide'.

Brady
Irish, meaning 'large-chested'.

Bradyn
(alt. Braden, Bradan)
Gaelic, meaning 'descendant of Bradan'.

Saints' names

Anselm
Bartholomew
Francis
Gabriel
Gregory
Jerome
Nicholas
Philip
Stephen
Thomas

Bram
Gaelic, meaning 'raven'.

Brando
Old Norse, meaning 'sword' or 'flaming torch'. Associated with movie star Marlon Brando.

Brandon
Old English, meaning 'gorse'.

Brandt
Old English, meaning 'beacon'.

Brannon
Gaelic, meaning 'raven'.

Branson
English, meaning 'son of Brand'.

B

B

Brant
Old English, meaning 'hill'.

Braulio
Greek, meaning 'shining'.

Brendan
Gaelic, meaning 'prince'.

Brennan
Gaelic, meaning 'teardrop'.

Brent
English, meaning 'hill'.

Brenton
English, meaning 'hill town'.

Brett
(alt. Bret)
English, meaning 'a Breton'.
Made popular by *Poison* lead
vocalist Bret Michaels.

Brian
Gaelic, meaning 'high' or
'noble'.

Brice
Latin, meaning 'speckled'.

Brier
French, meaning 'heather'.

Brock
Old English, meaning 'badger'.

Broderick
English, meaning 'ruler'.

Brody
Gaelic, meaning both 'ditch'
and 'brother'.

Brogan
Irish, meaning 'sturdy shoe'.

Bronwyn
Welsh, meaning 'white
breasted'.

Brook
English, meaning 'stream'.

Brooklyn
American, from the New York
City suburb of the same name.

Bruce
Scottish, meaning 'high' or
'noble'.

Bruno
Germanic, meaning 'brown'.

Bryant
English variant of Brian,
meaning 'high' or 'noble'.

Bryce
Scottish, meaning 'of Britain'.

Brycen
Scottish, meaning 'son of
Bryce'.

Bryden
Irish, meaning 'strong one'.

Bryson
Welsh, meaning 'descendant of Brice'.

Bubba
American, meaning 'boy'. The restaurant chain Bubba Gump Shrimp Co. takes its name from the characters of Benjamin Buford 'Bubba' Blue and Forrest Gump in the movie *Forrest Gump*.

Buck
American, meaning 'goat' or 'deer'.

Bud
(alt. Buddy)
American, meaning 'friend'.

Burdett
Middle English, meaning 'bird'.

Burke
French, meaning 'fortified settlement'.

Burl
French, meaning 'knotty wood'.

Buzz
American, from Busby, meaning 'village in the thicket'. Associated with the astronaut Buzz Aldrin.

Byron
Old English, meaning 'barn'. Made famous by the poet Lord Byron.

B

C Boys' names

C

Cabot
Old English, meaning 'to sail'.

Cade
(alt. Caden)
English, meaning 'round, lumpy'.

Cadence
Latin, meaning 'with rhythm'.

Cadogan
Welsh, meaning 'battle glory and honor'.

Caedmon
Celtic, meaning 'wise warrior'.

Caelan
Gaelic, meaning 'slender'.

Caerwyn
(alt. Carwyn, Gerwyn)
Welsh, meaning 'white fort' or 'settlement'.

Caesar
(alt. Cesar)
Latin, meaning 'head of hair'. Made famous by the first Roman emperor Julius Caesar.

Caetano
Portuguese, meaning 'from Gaeta, Italy'

Caiden
Arabic, meaning 'companion'.

Caillou
French, meaning 'pebble'.

Cain
Hebrew, meaning 'full of beauty'.

Cainan
Hebrew, meaning 'possessor' or 'purchaser'.

C

Cairo
Egyptian city.

Calder
Scottish, meaning 'rough waters'.

Caleb
(alt. Cal, Calen)
Hebrew, meaning 'dog'.

Calix
Greek, meaning 'very handsome'.

Callahan
Irish, meaning 'contention' or 'strife'.

Callum
Gaelic, meaning 'dove'.

Calvin
French, meaning 'little bald one'.

Camden
Gaelic, meaning 'winding valley'.

Cameron
Scottish Gaelic, meaning 'crooked nose'.

Camillo
Latin, meaning 'free born' or 'noble'.

Campbell
Scottish Gaelic, meaning 'crooked mouth'.

Canaan
Hebrew, meaning 'to be humbled'.

Candido
Latin, meaning 'candid' or 'honest'.

Cannon
French, meaning 'of the church'.

Canton
French, meaning 'dweller of corner'. Also the name given to areas of Switzerland.

Cappy
Italian, meaning 'lucky'.

Carden
Old English, meaning 'wool carder'.

Carey
Gaelic, meaning 'love'.

Carl
(alt. Carlo, Carlos)
Old Norse, meaning 'free man'.

Carlton
Old English, meaning 'free peasant settlement'.

C

Carmelo
Latin, meaning 'garden' or 'orchard'.

Carmen
Latin/Spanish, meaning 'song'.

Carmine
Latin, meaning 'song'.

Carnell
English, meaning 'defender of the castle'.

Carson
(alt. Carsten)
Scottish, meaning 'marsh-dwellers'.

Carter
Old English, meaning 'transporter of goods'.

Cary
Celtic, meaning 'love'. Old Celtic river name.

Case
(alt. Casey)
Irish Gaelic, meaning 'alert' or 'watchful'.

Cash
Latin, shortened form of Cassius, meaning 'empty, hollow'.

Casimer
Slavic, meaning 'famous destroyer of peace'.

Cason
Latin, from Cassius, meaning 'empty' or 'hollow'.

Casper
Persian, meaning 'treasurer'.

Caspian
English, meaning 'of the Caspy people'.

Cassidy
Gaelic, meaning 'curly haired'.

Cassius
(alt. Cassio)
Latin, meaning 'empty, hollow'. Legendary boxer Muhammad Ali's birth name was Cassius Clay.

Cathal
Celtic, meaning 'battle rule'.

Cato
Latin, meaning 'all-knowing'.

Cecil
Latin, meaning 'blind'.

Cedar
English, name of an evergreen tree.

Cedric
Welsh, meaning 'spectacular bounty'.

C

TV personality names

Billy (Bush)
Conon (O'Brien)
Drew (Carey)
Jay (Leno)
Jeff (Probst)
Joel (McHale)

Jon (Stewart)
Mario (Lopez)
Nick (Cannon)
Ryan (Seacrest)
Stephen (Colbert)
Tom (Bergeron)

Celestino
Spanish/Italian meaning
'heavenly'.

Chad
(alt. Chadrick)
Old English, meaning 'warlike,
warrior'.

Chaim
Hebrew, meaning 'life'.

Champion
English, from the word
'champion'.

Chance
English, from the word
'chance, meaning 'good
fortune'.

Chandler
Old English, meaning 'candle
maker and seller'.

Charles
(alt. Charlie)
Old German, meaning 'free
man'.

Chase
Old French, meaning
'huntermen'.

Chaska
Native American name usually
given to first son.

Che
Spanish, shortened form of
José. Made famous by Che
Guevara.

Chesley
Old English, meaning 'camp on
the meadow'.

Chester
Latin, meaning 'camp of
soldiers'.

C

Chima
Old English, meaning 'hilly land'.

Christian
English, from the word 'Christian'.

Christopher
(alt. Chris, Christophe)
Greek, meaning 'bearing Christ inside'.

Cian
Irish, meaning 'ancient'.

Ciaran
Irish, meaning 'black'.

Cicero
Latin, meaning 'chickpea'. Also the Roman philosopher and orator.

Cimarron
City in western Kansas.

Ciprian
Latin, meaning 'from Cyprus'.

Ciro
Spanish, meaning 'sun'.

Clancy
Old Irish, meaning 'red warrior'.

Clarence
Latin, meaning 'one who lives near the river Clare'.

Clark
Latin, meaning 'clerk'.

Claude
(alt. Claudie, Claudio, Claudius)
Latin, meaning 'lame'.

Claus
Variant of Nicholas, meaning 'people of victory'.

Clay
English, from the word 'clay'.

Clement
(alt. Clem)
Latin, meaning 'merciful'.

Cleo
Greek, meaning 'glory'.

Cletus
Greek, meaning 'illustrious'.

Cliff
(alt. Clifford, Clifton)
English, from the word 'cliff'.

Clint
(alt. Clinton)
Old English, meaning 'fenced settlement'.

Clive
Old English, meaning 'cliff' or 'slope'.

C

Clyde
Scottish, from the river in Glasgow.

Coby
(alt. Cody, Colby)
Irish, son of Oda.

Colden
Old English, meaning 'dark valley'.

Cole
(alt. Coley)
Old French, meaning 'coal black'.

Colin
Gaelic, meaning 'young creature'.

Colson
Old English, meaning 'coal black'.

Colton
English, meaning 'swarthy'.

Columbus
Latin, meaning 'dove'. Explorer Christopher Columbus is credited with discovering America.

Colwyn
Welsh, from the river in Wales.

Conan
Gaelic, meaning 'wolf'.

Conley
Gaelic, meaning 'sensible'.

Connell
(alt. Connolly)
Irish, meaning 'high' or 'mighty'.

Connor
(alt. Conrad, Conroy)
Irish, meaning 'lover of hounds'.

Constant
(alt. Constantine)
English, from the word 'constant'.

Cooper
Old English, meaning 'barrel maker'.

Corban
Hebrew, meaning 'dedicated and belonging to God'.

Corbett
(alt. Corbin, Corby)
Norman French, meaning 'young crow'.

Cordell
Old English, meaning 'cord maker'.

Corey
Gaelic, meaning 'hill hollow'.

C

Uncommon three syllable names

Alastair
Barnaby
Dominic
Elijah
Elliot
Gideon
Gregory
Nathaniel
Reginald
Roderick
Theodore

Corin
Latin, meaning 'spear'.

Cormac
Gaelic, meaning 'impure son'. American writer Cormac McCarthy is the author of modern classics *No Country for Old Men* and *The Road*.

Cornelius
(alt. Cornell)
Latin, meaning 'horn'.

Cortez
Spanish, meaning 'courteous'.

Corwin
Old English, meaning 'heart's friend' or 'companion'.

Cosimo
(alt. Cosme, Cosmo)
Italian, meaning 'order' or 'beauty'.

Coty
French, meaning 'riverbank'.

Coulter
English, meaning 'young horse'.

Courtney
Old English, meaning 'domain of Curtis'.

Covey
English, meaning 'flock of birds'.

Cowan
Gaelic, meaning 'hollow in the hill'.

Craig
Welsh, meaning 'rock'.

Crispin
Latin, meaning 'curly haired'.

Croix
French, meaning 'cross'.

Cruz
Spanish, meaning 'cross'.

C

Curran
Gaelic, meaning 'dagger' or 'hero'.

Curtis
(alt. Curt)
Old French, meaning 'courteous'. Made popular by screen legend Tony Curtis.

Cutler
Old English, meaning 'knife maker'.

Cyprian
English, meaning 'from Cyprus'.

Cyril
Greek, meaning 'master' or 'Lord'.

Cyrus
Persian, meaning 'Lord'.

Popular American names for boys

Aiden	Jayden
Braydon	Landon
Cooper	Logan
Elijah	Mason
Grayson	Peyton

D
Boys' names

Dafydd
Welsh, meaning 'beloved'.

Daichi
Japanese, meaning 'great wisdom'.

Daisuke
Japanese, meaning 'lionhearted'.

Dakari
African, meaning 'happy'.

Dakota
Native American, meaning 'friend' or 'ally'.

Dale
Old English, meaning 'valley'.

Dallin
English, meaning 'dweller in the valley'.

Dalton
English, meaning 'town in the valley'. Actor Timothy Dalton is known for his portrayal of *James Bond*.

Daly
Gaelic, meaning 'assembly'.

Damarion
Greek, meaning 'gentle'.

Damian
(alt. Damon)
Greek, meaning 'to tame, subdue'.

Dane
Old English, meaning 'from Denmark'.

Daniel
(alt. Dan, Danny)
Hebrew, meaning 'God is my judge'.

D

Dante
Latin, meaning 'lasting'. Associated with the Italian 13th century poet Dante Alighieri.

Darby
Irish, meaning 'without envy'.

Darcy
Gaelic, meaning 'dark'. Associated with Jane Austen's Mr Darcy.

Dario
(alt. Darius)
Greek, meaning 'kingly'.

Darnell
Old English, meaning 'the hidden spot'.

Darragh
Irish, meaning 'dark oak'.

Darrell
(alt. Daryl)
Old English, meaning 'open'.

Darren
(alt. Darrian)
Gaelic, meaning 'great'.

Darrick
Old German, meaning 'power of the tribe'.

Darshan
Hindi, meaning 'vision'.

Darwin
Old English, meaning 'dear friend'.

Dash
(alt. Dashawn)
American, meaning 'enlightened one'.

Dashiell
French, meaning 'page boy'.

David
(alt. Dave, Davey, Davie, Davian)
Hebrew, meaning 'beloved'.

Davis
Old English, meaning 'son of David'.

Dawson
Old English, meaning 'son of David'.

Dax
(alt. Daxton)
French, from the town in southwestern France.

Dayal
Indian, meaning 'kind'.

Dayton
Old English, meaning 'David's place'.

Dean
Old English, meaning 'valley'.

D

Declan
Irish, meaning 'full of goodness'.

Dedric
Old English, meaning 'gifted ruler'.

Deegan
(alt. Deagon, Daegan)
Irish, meaning 'black-haired'.

Deepak
(alt. Deepan)
Indian, meaning 'illumination'.

Del
(alt. Delano, Delbert, Dell)
Old English, meaning 'bright shining one'.

Demetrius
Greek, meaning 'harvest lover'. One of the main characters in Shakespeare's play *A Midsummer Night's Dream*.

Dempsey
Irish, meaning 'proud'.

Denham
(alt. Denholm)
Old English, meaning 'valley settlement'.

Dennis
(alt. Denny, Denton)
English, meaning 'follower of Dionysius'.

Old name, new fashion?

Augustus
Bertrand
Edgar
Felix
Gilbert
Hector
Jasper
Norris
Percival
Reginald
Sebastian
Theodore
Winston

Denver
Old English, meaning 'green valley'. City in Colorado.

Denzil
(alt. Denzel)
English, meaning 'fort'.

Deon
Greek, meaning 'of Zeus'.

Derek
English, meaning 'power of the tribe'.

Dermot
Irish, meaning 'free man'.

D

Desmond
Irish, meaning 'from south Munster'.

Destin
French, meaning 'destiny'.

Devyn
Irish, meaning 'poet'.

Dewey
(alt. Dewi)
Welsh, meaning 'beloved'.

Dexter
(alt. Dex)
Latin, meaning 'right-handed'.

Dick
(alt. Dickie, Dickon)
From Richard, meaning 'powerful leader'.

Didier
French, meaning 'much desired'.

Diego
Spanish, meaning 'supplanter'.

Dietrich
Old German, meaning 'power of the tribe'.

Diggory
English, meaning 'dyke'.

Dilbert
English, meaning 'day-bright'. Main character in the comic strip of the same name.

Dimitri
(alt. Dimitrios, Dimitris)
Greek, meaning 'prince'.

Dino
Diminutive of Dean, meaning 'valley'.

Dion
Greek, short form of Dionysius.

Dirk
Variant of Derek, meaning 'power of the tribe'.

Dobbin
(alt. Dobby)
Diminutive of Robert, meaning 'bright fame'.

Dominic
Latin, meaning 'Lord'.

Donald
(alt. Don, Donal, Donaldo)
Gaelic, meaning 'great chief'.

Donato
Italian, meaning 'gift'.

Donnell
(alt. Donnie, Donny)
Gaelic, meaning 'world fighter'.

Donovan
Gaelic, meaning 'dark-haired chief'.

Doran
Gaelic, meaning 'exile'.

Dorian
Greek, meaning 'descendant of Doris'.

Douglas
(alt. Dougal, Dougie)
Scottish, meaning 'black river'.

Draco
Latin, meaning 'dragon'. Made popular by the character Draco Malfoy in the Harry Potter series.

Drake
Greek, meaning 'dragon'.

Drew
Greek, from Andrew, meaning 'man' or 'warrior'.

Dudley
Old English, meaning 'people's field'.

Duff
Gaelic, meaning 'swarthy'.

Duke
Latin, meaning 'leader'.

Duncan
Scottish, meaning 'dark warrior'.

Dustin
(alt. Dusty)
French, meaning 'brave warrior'.

Dwayne
Irish Gaelic, meaning 'swarthy'.

Dwight
Flemish, meaning 'blond'.

Dwyer
Gaelic, meaning 'dark wise one'.

Dylan
(alt. Delyn, Dillon)
Welsh, meaning 'son of the sea'.

E Boys' names

Eamon
(alt. Eames)
Irish, meaning 'wealthy protector'.

Earl
(alt. Earle, Errol)
English, meaning 'nobleman, warrior'.

Ebenezer
(alt. Ebb)
Hebrew, meaning 'stone of help'.

Ed
(alt. Edd, Eddie, Eddy)
Old English, from Edward, meaning 'wealthy guard'.

Edgar
(alt. Elgar)
Old English, meaning 'wealthy spear'. Gothic poet Edgar Allen Poe wrote *'The Raven'* amongst others.

Edison
English, meaning 'son of Edward'.

Edmund
English, meaning 'wealthy protector'.

Edric
Old English, meaning 'rich and powerful'.

Edsel
Old German, meaning 'noble'.

Edward
(alt. Eduardo)
Old English, meaning 'wealthy guard'.

Edwin
English, meaning 'wealthy friend'.

E

Efrain
Hebrew, meaning 'fruitful'.

Egan
Irish, meaning 'fire'.

Einar
Old Norse, meaning 'battle leader'.

Eladio
Greek, meaning 'Greek'.

Elam
Hebrew, meaning 'eternal'.

Elbert
Old English, meaning 'famous'.

Eldon
Old English, meaning 'Ella's hill'.

Eldred
(alt. Eldridge)
Old English, meaning 'old venerable counsel'.

Elgin
Old English, meaning 'high minded'.

Eli
(alt. Eliah)
Hebrew, meaning 'high'.

Elias
(alt. Elijah)
Hebrew, meaning 'the Lord is my God'.

Elio
Spanish, meaning 'the Lord is my God'.

Ellery
Old English, meaning 'elder tree'.

Elliott
Variant of Elio, meaning 'the Lord is my God'.

Ellis
Welsh variant of Elio, meaning 'the Lord is my God'.

Ellison
English, meaning 'son of Ellis'.

Elmer
(alt. Elmo)
Old English, meaning 'noble'; Arabic, meaning 'aristocratic'.

Elon
Hebrew, meaning 'oak tree'.

Elroy
French, meaning 'king'.

Elton
Old English, meaning 'Ella's town'.

Elvin
English, meaning 'elf-like'.

E

Elvis
Figure in Norse mythology. Made famous by the singer Elvis Presley.

Emanuel
Hebrew, meaning 'God is with us'.

Emeric
German, meaning 'work rule'.

Emile
(alt. Emiliano, Emilio)
Latin, meaning 'eager'.

Emlyn
Welsh, from the UK town of the same name.

Emmett
English, meaning 'universal'.

Emrys
Welsh, meaning 'immortal'.

Enoch
Hebrew, meaning 'dedicated'.

Enrico
(alt. Enrique)
Italian form of Henry, meaning 'home ruler'.

Enzo
Italian, short for Lorenzo, meaning 'laurel'.

Eoghan
(alt. Eoin)
Irish form of Owen, meaning 'well born' or 'noble'.

Ephron
(alt. Effron)
Hebrew, meaning 'dust'.

Erasmo
(alt. Erasmus)
Greek, meaning 'to love'.

Eric
Old Norse, meaning 'ruler'.

Ernest
(alt. Ernesto, Ernie, Ernst)
Old German, meaning 'serious'. Author Ernest Hemingway wrote the novel *The Old Man and the Sea*, amongst others.

Erskine
Scottish, meaning 'high cliff'.

Erwin
Old English, meaning 'boar friend'.

Ethan
(alt. Etienne)
Hebrew, meaning 'long lived'.

Eugene
Greek, meaning 'well born'.

E

Evan
Welsh, meaning 'God is good'.

Everard
Old English, meaning 'strong boar'.

Everett
English, meaning 'strong boar'.

Ewald
(alt. Ewan, Ewell)
Old English, from Owen, meaning 'well born' or 'noble'.

Exton
English, meaning 'on the river Exe'.

Ezra
Hebrew, meaning 'helper'.

Popular names of English and Scottish Kings and Consorts

Alexander	James
Charles	Richard
Edward	Robert
George	Stephen
Henry	William

F

Boys' names

Fabian
(alt. *Fabien, Fabio*)
Latin, meaning 'one who grows beans'.

Fabrice
(alt. *Fabrizio*)
Latin, meaning 'works with his hands'.

Faisal
Arabic, meaning 'resolute'.

Faron
Spanish, meaning 'pharaoh'.

Farrell
Gaelic, meaning 'hero'.

Faulkner
Latin, from 'falcon'.

Faustino
Latin, meaning 'fortunate'.

Felipe
(alt. *Filippo*)
Spanish, meaning 'lover of horses'.

Felix
(alt. *Felice*)
Italian/Latin, meaning 'happy'. Felix the Cat was first developed as a cartoon during the silent movie era.

Fennel
Latin, name of a herb.

Ferdinand
(alt. *Fernando*)
Old German, meaning 'bold voyager'.

Fergus
(alt. *Ferguson*)
Gaelic, meaning 'supreme man'.

F

Names of poets

Alfred (Lord Tennyson)
Allen (Ginsberg)
Dylan (Thomas)
Geoffrey (Chaucer)
Langston (Hughes)

Ralph (Waldo Emerson)
Robert (Burns)
Seamus (Heaney)
Walt (Whitman)
William (Wordsworth)

Ferris
Gaelic, meaning 'rock'.

Fidel
Latin, meaning 'faithful'.

Finbar
Gaelic, meaning 'fair head'.

Finian
Gaelic, meaning 'fair'.

Finlay
(alt. Finley, Finn)
Gaelic, meaning 'fair-haired courageous one'.

Finnegan
Gaelic, meaning 'fair'.

Fintan
Gaelic, meaning 'little fair one'.

Flavio
Latin, meaning 'yellow hair'.

Florencio
(alt. Florentino)
Latin, meaning 'from Florence'.

Florian
(alt. Florin)
Slavic/Latin, meaning 'flower'.

Floyd
Welsh, meaning 'gray haired'.

Flynn
Gaelic, meaning 'with a ruddy complexion'.

Fortunato
Italian, meaning 'lucky'.

Forrest
(alt. Forest)
Old French, meaning 'woodsman'. Made popular by the movie *Forrest Gump*.

F

Foster
Old English, meaning 'woodsman'.

Fotini
(alt. Fotis)
Greek, meaning 'light'.

Francesco
(alt. Francis, Francisco, Franco, François)
Latin, meaning 'from France'.

Frank
(alt. Frankie, Franklin, Franz)
Middle English, meaning 'free landholder'.

Fraser
(alt. Frasier)
Scottish, meaning 'of the forest men'. Frasier was a 90s sitcom revolving around main character Dr Frasier Crane.

Frederick
(alt. Fred, Freddie, Freddy)
Old German, meaning 'peaceful ruler'.

Furman
Old German, meaning 'ferryman'.

Popular African names for boys and girls

Abiba	Jelani
Chike	Kanene
Ebere	Keisha
Faizah	Razi
Fola	Salim

G

G

Boys' names

Gabino
Latin, meaning 'God is my strength'.

Gabriel
(alt. Gale)
Hebrew, meaning 'hero of God'. An archangel of God.

Gael
(alt. Gale)
English, old reference to the Celts.

Gage
(alt. Gaige)
Old French, meaning 'pledge'.

Galen
Greek, meaning 'healer'.

Galileo
Italian, meaning 'from Galilee'.

Ganesh
Hindi, meaning 'Lord of the throngs'. One of the Hindu deities.

Gannon
Irish, meaning 'fair skinned'.

Gareth
(alt. Garth)
Welsh, meaning 'gentle'.

Garfield
Old English, meaning 'spear field'. Also the name of the cartoon cat.

Garland
English, as in 'garland of flowers'.

Garnet
English, precious stone red in color.

G

Garrett
(alt. Garet)
Germanic, meaning 'strength of the spear'.

Gary
(alt. Garry, Geary)
Old English, meaning 'spear'.

Gaspar
(alt. Gaspard)
Persian, meaning 'treasurer'.

Gaston
From the region in the south of France.

Gavin
(alt. Gawain)
Scottish/Welsh, meaning 'little falcon'.

Gene
Greek, shortened form of Eugene, meaning 'well born'. Made popular by actor and dancer Gene Kelly.

Gennaro
Italian, meaning 'of Janus'.

Geoffrey
(alt. Geoff)
Old German, meaning 'peace'.

George
(alt. Giorgio)
Greek, meaning 'farmer'.

Gerald
(alt. Geraldo, Gerard, Gerardo, Gerhard)
Old German, meaning 'spear ruler'.

Geronimo
Italian, meaning 'sacred name'.

Gerry
English, meaning 'independent'.

Gert
Old German, meaning 'strong spear'.

Gervase
Old German, meaning 'with honor'.

Giacomo
Italian, meaning 'God's son'.

Gibson
English, meaning 'son of Gilbert'.

Gideon
Hebrew, meaning 'tree cutter'.

Gilbert
(alt. Gilberto)
French, meaning 'bright promise'.

Giles
Greek, meaning 'small goat'.

Gino
Italian, meaning 'well born'.

Giovanni
Italian form of John, meaning 'God is gracious'.

Giulio
Italian, meaning 'youthful'.

Giuseppe
Italian form of Joseph, meaning 'Jehovah increases'.

Glen
(alt. Glenn, Glyn)
English, from the word 'glen'. Glenn Miller was a world-renowned big band director and composer.

Godfrey
German, meaning 'peace of God'.

Gordon
Gaelic, meaning 'large fortification'.

Gottlieb
German, meaning 'good love'.

Graeme
(alt. Graham)
English, meaning 'gravelled area'.

Grant
English, from the word 'grant'.

Granville
English, meaning 'gravelly town'.

Gray
(alt. Grey)
English, from the word 'gray'.

Grayson
English, meaning 'son of gray'.

Green
English, from the word 'green'.

Gregory
(alt. Greg, Gregorio, Grieg)
English, meaning 'watcher'.

Griffin
English, from the word 'griffin'.

Names from ancient Rome

Brutus
Caesar
Julius
Lucius
Marcus
Maximus
Nero
Rufus
Titus

G

Guido
Italian, meaning 'guide'.

Guillaume
French form of William,
meaning 'strong protector'.

Gulliver
English, meaning 'glutton'.
Made popular after the
publication of *Gulliver's Travels*
by Jonathan Swift.

Gunther
German, meaning 'warrior'.

Gurpreet
Indian, meaning 'love of the
teacher'.

Gustave
(alt. Gus)
Scandinavian, meaning
'royal staff'.

Guy
English, from the word 'guy'.

Gwyn
Welsh, meaning 'white'.

H

Boys' names

Habib
Arabic, meaning 'beloved one'.

Haden
(alt. Haiden)
English, meaning 'hedged valley'.

Hades
Greek, meaning 'sightless'. Name of the underworld in Greek mythology.

Hadrian
From Hadria, a north Italian city.

Hadwin
Old English, meaning 'friend in war'.

Hakeem
Arabic, meaning 'wise and insightful'.

Hal
(alt. Hale)
English, nickname for Henry, meaning 'home ruler'.

Hamid
Arabic, meaning 'praiseworthy'.

Hamilton
Old English, meaning 'flat topped hill'.

Hamish
Scottish form of James, meaning 'he who supplants'.

Hampus
Swedish form of Homer, meaning 'pledge'.

Hamza
Arabic, meaning 'lamb'.

H

Han
(alt. Hannes, Hans)
Scandinavian, meaning 'the
Lord is gracious'.

Hank
German, form of Henry,
meaning 'home ruler'.

Hansel
German, meaning 'the Lord is
gracious'. *Hansel and Gretel*
is a children's fairy tale by the
Brothers Grimm.

Hardy
English, meaning 'tough'.

Harlan
English, meaning 'dweller by
the boundary wood'.

Harland
Old English, meaning 'army
land'.

Harley
Old English, meaning 'hare
meadow'.

Harmon
Old German, meaning 'soldier'.

Harold
Scandinavian, meaning 'army
ruler'.

Harry
Old German, form of Henry,
meaning 'home ruler'.

Hart
Old English, meaning 'stag'.

Harvey
Old English, meaning 'strong
and worthy'.

Haskell
Hebrew, meaning 'intellect'.

Hassan
Arabic, meaning 'handsome'.

Haydn
(alt. Hayden)
Old English, meaning 'hedged
valley'.

Names from ancient Greece

Aesop
Demetrius
Erasmus
Georgios
Homer
Jason
Lysandos
Nikolaos
Pyrrhus
Theodore

Heart
English, from the word 'heart'.

Heath
English, meaning 'heath' or 'moor'.

Heathcliff
English, meaning 'cliff near a heath'. Made famous by Emily Bronte's novel *Wuthering Heights*.

Heber
Hebrew, meaning 'partner'.

Hector
Greek, meaning 'steadfast'.

Henry
(alt. Henri, Hendrik, Hendrix) Old German, meaning 'home ruler'.

Henson
English, meaning 'son of Henry'.

Herbert
(alt. Bert, Herb, Heriberto) Old German, meaning 'illustrious warrior'.

Herman
(alt. Herminio, Hermon) Old German, meaning 'soldier'.

Hermes
Greek, meaning 'messenger'.

Herschel
Yiddish, meaning 'deer'.

Hezekiah
Hebrew, meaning 'God gives strength'.

Hideki
Japanese, meaning 'excellent trees'.

Hideo
Japanese, meaning 'excellent name'.

Hilario
Latin, meaning 'cheerful, happy'.

Hilary
English, meaning 'cheerful'.

Hillel
Hebrew, meaning 'greatly praised'.

Hilliard
Old German, meaning 'battle guard'.

Hilton
Old English, meaning 'hill settlement'.

H

H

Hiram
Hebrew, meaning 'exalted brother'.

Hiro
Spanish, meaning 'sacred name'.

Hiroshi
Japanese, meaning 'generous'.

Hirsch
Yiddish, meaning 'deer'.

Hobart
English, meaning 'bright and shining intellect'.

Hodge
English, meaning 'son of Roger'.

Hogan
Gaelic, meaning 'youth'. Became well known after the success of sitcom *Hogan's Heroes* in the 60s. Also made famous by wrestler Hulk Hogan.

Holden
English, meaning 'deep valley'.

Hollis
Old English, meaning 'holly tree'.

Homer
Greek, meaning 'pledge'.

Honorius
Latin, meaning 'honorable'.

Horace
Latin, name of the Roman poet.

Houston
Old English, meaning 'Hugh's town'.

Howard
Old English, meaning 'noble watchman'.

Howell
Welsh, meaning 'eminent and remarkable'.

Hoyt
Norse, meaning 'spirit' or 'soul'.

Hristo
From Christo, meaning 'follower of Christ'.

Hubert
German, meaning 'bright and shining intellect'.

Hudson
Old English, meaning 'son of Hugh'.

H

Hugh
(alt. Huw)
Old German, meaning 'soul, mind and intellect'.

Humbert
Old German, meaning 'famous giant'. Made famous by the paedophile protagonist of Vladimir Nabokov's *Lolita*.

Humphrey
Old German, meaning 'peaceful warrior'.

Hunter
English, from the word 'hunter'.

Hurley
Gaelic, meaning 'sea tide'.

Huxley
Old English, meaning 'Hugh's meadow'.

Hyrum
Hebrew, meaning 'exalted brother'.

Names with positive meanings

Auden (Friend)
Basim (Smile)
Dustin (Brave)
Ervin (Beautiful)
Gene (Noble)

Jamal (Handsome)
Jay (Happy)
Lucas (Light)
Tate (Cheerful)
Tova (Good)

I Boys' names

Iago
Spanish, meaning 'he who supplants'.

Ian
(alt. Ion)
Gaelic, variant of John, meaning 'God is gracious'.

Ianto
Welsh, meaning 'gift of God'.

Ibrahim
Arabic, meaning 'father of many'.

Ichabod
Hebrew, meaning 'glory is good'.

Ichiro
Japanese, meaning 'firstborn son'.

Idris
Welsh, meaning 'fiery leader'.

Girls' names for boys (male spellings)

Casey
Darcy
Gene
Kay
Kelly
Kelsey
Madison
Nat
Sandy
Sasha

I

Ifan
Welsh variant of John, meaning 'God is gracious'.

Ignacio
Latin, meaning 'ardent' or 'burning'.

Ignatz
German, meaning 'fiery'.

Igor
Russian, meaning 'Ing's soldier'.

Ikaika
Hawaiian, meaning 'strong'.

Ike
Hebrew, short for Isaac, meaning 'laughter'.

Ilan
Hebrew, meaning 'tree'.

Ilias
Variant of Elijah, Hebrew, meaning 'the Lord is my God'.

Imanol
Hebrew, meaning 'God is with us'.

Indiana
Latin, meaning 'from India'.

Indigo
English, describing a deep blue color.

Indio
Spanish, meaning 'indigenous people'.

Ingo
Danish, meaning 'meadow'.

Inigo
Spanish, meaning 'fiery'.

Ioannis
Greek, meaning 'the Lord is gracious'.

Ira
Hebrew, meaning 'full grown and watchful'.

Irvin
(alt. Irving, Irwin)
Gaelic, meaning 'green and fresh water'.

Place names

Adrian
Austin
Bradley
Brooklyn
Cheyenne
Dallas
Glen
Houston
Paris
Tay
Tennessee

I

Isaac
(alt. Isaak)
Hebrew, meaning 'laughter'.

Isadore
(alt. Isidore, Isidro)
Greek, meaning 'gift of Isis'.

Isai
(alt. Isaiah, Isaias, Izaiah)
Arabic, meaning 'protection and security'.

Iser
Yiddish, meaning 'God wrestler'.

Ishmael
(alt. Ismael)
Hebrew, meaning 'God listens'. The narrator and protagonist of *Moby Dick*, by Herman Melville.

Israel
Hebrew, meaning 'God perseveres'. Also the name of the country.

Istvan
Hungarian variant of Stephen, meaning 'crowned'.

Itai
Hebrew, meaning 'the Lord is with me'.

Ivan
Hebrew, meaning 'God is gracious'.

Ivanhoe
Russian, meaning 'God is gracious'. Also name of the novel by Walter Scott.

Ivey
English, variant of Ivy.

Ivo
French, from the word 'yves', meaning 'yew tree'.

Ivor
Scandinavian, meaning 'yew'.

Ivory
English, from the word 'ivory'.

Long names

Alexander
Bartholomew
Christopher
Demetrius
Giovanni
Maximillian
Montgomery
Nathaniel
Sebastian
Zachariah

127

J

Boys' names

Jabari
Swahili, meaning 'valiant'.

Jabez
Hebrew, meaning 'borne in pain'.

Jace
(alt. Jaece, Jase, Jayce)
Hebrew, meaning 'healer'.

Jacek
(alt. Jacirto)
African, meaning 'hyacinth'.

Jack
(alt. Jackie, Jacky)
From the Hebrew John, meaning 'God is gracious'.

Jackson
(alt. Jaxon)
English, meaning 'son of Jack'.

Jacob
(alt. Jaco, Jacobo, Jago)
Hebrew, meaning 'he who supplants'.

Jacques
(alt. Jaquez)
French form of Jack, meaning 'God is gracious'.

Jaden
(alt. Jaden, Jadyn, Jaeden, Jaiden, Jaidyn, Jayden, Jaydin)
Hebrew, meaning 'Jehovah has heard'.

Jafar
Arabic, meaning 'stream'.

Jagger
Old English, meaning 'one who cuts'. Made famous by *Rolling Stones* singer Mick Jagger.

J

Jaheem
(alt. Jaheim)
Hebrew, meaning 'raised up'.

Jahir
Hindi, meaning 'jewel'.

Jaime
Variant for James, meaning 'he who supplants'. 'J'aime' is also French for 'I love'.

Jair
(alt. Jairo)
Hebrew, meaning 'God enlightens'.

Jake
Shortened form of Jacob, meaning 'he who supplants'.

Jalen
Greek, meaning 'healer' or 'tranquil'.

Jali
Swahili, meaning 'musician'.

Jalon
Greek, meaning 'healer' or 'tranquil'.

Jamaal
(alt. Jamal)
Arabic, meaning 'handsome'.

Jamar
(alt. Jamarcus, Jamari, Jamarion, Jamir)
Modern variant of Jamaal, meaning 'handsome'.

James
English, meaning 'he who supplants'.

Jameson
(alt. Jamison)
English, meaning 'son of James'.

Jamie
(alt. Jamey, Jaimie)
Nickname for James, meaning 'he who supplants'.

Jamil
Arabic, meaning 'handsome'.

Jamin
Hebrew, meaning 'son of the right hand'.

Jan
(alt. Janko, János)
Slavic, from John meaning 'the Lord is gracious'.

Janus
Latin, meaning 'gateway'. Roman god of doors, beginnings and endings.

Japhet
(alt. Japheth)
Hebrew, meaning 'comely'.

J

Jared
(alt. Jarem, Jaren, Jaret, Jarod, Jarrod)
Hebrew, meaning 'descending'.

Jarlath
Gaelic, from Iarlaith, from Saint Iarfhlaith.

Jarom
Greek, meaning 'to raise and exalt'.

Jarrell
Variant of Gerald, meaning 'spear ruler'.

Jarrett
Old English, meaning 'spear-brave'.

Short names

Al
Ben
Dai
Ed
Jay
Jon
Max
Rio
Sam
Ty

Jarvis
Old German, meaning 'with honor'.

Jason
Greek, meaning 'healer'.

Jasper
Greek, meaning 'treasure holder'.

Javen
Arabic, meaning 'youth'.

Javier
Spanish, meaning 'bright'.

Jay
Latin, meaning 'jaybird'.

Jaylan
(alt. Jaylen)
Greek, meaning 'healer'.

Jeevan
Indian, meaning 'life'.

Jefferson
English, meaning 'son of Jeffrey'.

Jeffrey
(alt. Jeff)
Old German, meaning 'peace'.

Jensen
Scandinavian, meaning 'son of Jan'.

J

Jeremy
(alt. Jem)
Hebrew, meaning 'the Lord exalts'.

Jeriah
Hebrew, meaning 'Jehovah has seen'.

Jericho
Arabic, meaning 'city of the moon'. Site of the epic biblical Battle of Jericho.

Jermaine
Latin, meaning 'brotherly'.

Jerome
Greek, meaning 'sacred name'.

Jerry
English, from Gerald, meaning 'spear ruler'.

Jesse
Hebrew, meaning 'the Lord exists'.

Jesus
Hebrew, meaning 'the Lord is Salvation' and the Son of God.

Jet
(alt. Jett)
English, meaning 'black gemstone'.

Jethro
Hebrew, meaning 'eminent'.

Jim
(alt. Jimmy)
From James, meaning 'he who supplants'.

Jiri
(alt. Jiro)
Greek, meaning 'farmer'.

Joachim
Hebrew, meaning 'established by God'.

Joah
(alt. João)
Hebrew, meaning 'God is gracious' .

Joaquin
Hebrew, meaning 'established by God'. Academy Award winner Joaquin Phoenix was originally called 'Leaf' at birth.

Joe
(alt. Joey, Johan, Johannes, Jomar)
Shortened form of Joseph, meaning 'Jehovah increases'.

Joel
Hebrew, meaning 'Jehovah is the Lord'.

J

John
Hebrew, meaning 'God is gracious'.

Johnny
(alt. Jon, Jonny)
From Jonathan, meaning 'gift of God'.

Jolyon
From Julian, meaning 'young'.

Jonah
(alt. Jonas)
Hebrew, meaning 'dove'.

Jonathan
(alt. Johnathan, Johnathon, Jonathon, Jonty)
Hebrew, meaning 'God is gracious'.

Jordan
(alt. Jory, Judd)
Hebrew, meaning 'down-flowing'.

Jorge
From George, meaning 'farmer'.

José
Spanish variant of Joseph, meaning 'God increases'.

Joseph
(alt. Joss)
Hebrew, meaning 'God increases'.

Josh
Shortened form of Joshua, meaning 'Jehovah is salvation'.

Joshua
(alt. Joshué)
Hebrew, meaning 'Jehovah is salvation'.

Josiah
Hebrew, meaning 'God helps'.

Jovan
Latin, meaning 'the supreme God'.

Joyce
Latin, meaning 'joy'.

Juan
Spanish variant of John, meaning 'God is gracious'.

Jubal
Hebrew, meaning 'ram's horn'.

Jude
Hebrew, meaning 'praise' or 'thanks'.

Judson
Variant of Jude, meaning 'praise' or 'thanks'.

Jules
From Julian, meaning 'Jove's child'.

J

Julian
(alt. Julien, Julio)
Greek, meaning 'Jove's child'.

Junior
Latin, meaning 'the younger one'.

Junius
Latin, meaning 'young'.

Jupiter
Latin, meaning 'the supreme God'. Jupiter was king of the Roman gods and the god of thunder.

Juraj
Hebrew, meaning 'God is my judge'.

Jurgen
Greek, meaning 'farmer'.

Justice
English, from the word 'justice'.

Justin
(alt. Justus)
Latin, meaning 'just and upright'.

Juwan
Hebrew, meaning 'the Lord is gracious'.

'Bad boy' names

Ace
Arnie
Axel
Bruce
Buzz
Conan
Guy
Rhett
Spike
Tyson

K Boys' names

Kabelo
African, meaning 'gift'.

Kade
Scottish, meaning 'from the wetlands'.

Kadeem
Arabic, meaning 'one who serves'.

Kaden
(alt. Kadin, Kaeden, Kaedin, Kaiden)
Arabic, meaning 'companion'.

Kadir
Arabic, meaning 'capable and competent'.

Kahekili
Hawaiian, meaning 'the thunder'.

Kahlil
Arabic, meaning 'friend'.

Kai
Greek, meaning 'keeper of the keys'.

Kaito
Japanese, meaning 'ocean and sake dipper'. One of the most popular names for little boys in Japan.

Kalani
Hawaiian, meaning 'sky'.

Kale
German, meaning 'free man'.

Kaleb
Hebrew, meaning 'dog' or 'aggressive'.

Kalen
(alt. Kaelen, Kalan)
Gaelic, meaning 'uncertain'.

Kaleo
Hawaiian, meaning 'the voice'.

K

Kalil
Arabic, meaning 'friend'.

Kalvin
French, meaning 'bald'.

Kamari
Indian, meaning 'the enemy of desire'.

Kamden
English, meaning 'winding valley'.

Kamil
Arabic, meaning 'perfection'.

Kane
Gaelic, meaning 'little battler'.

Kani
Hawaiian, meaning 'sound'.

Kanye
African town in Botswana. Made popular by rapper Kanye West.

Kareem
(alt. Karim)
Arabic, meaning 'generous'.

Karl
(alt. Karson)
Old German, meaning 'free man'.

Kasey
(alt. Kacey)
Irish, meaning 'alert'.

Kaspar
Persian, meaning 'treasurer'.

Kavon
Gaelic, meaning 'handsome'.

Kayden
Arabic, meaning 'companion'.

Kazimierz
Polish, meaning 'declares peace'.

Kazuki
Japanese, meaning 'radiant hope'.

Kazuo
Japanese, meaning 'harmonious man'.

Keagan
(alt. Keegan, Kegan)
Gaelic, meaning 'small flame'.

Keane
Gaelic, meaning 'fighter'.

Keanu
Hawaiian, meaning 'breeze'. Made famous by actor Keanu Reeves.

Keary
Gaelic, meaning 'black-haired'.

Keaton
English, meaning 'place of hawks'.

K

Keeler
Gaelic, meaning 'beautiful and graceful'.

Keenan
(alt. Kenan)
Gaelic, meaning 'little ancient one'.

Keiji
Japanese, meaning 'govern with discretion'.

Keir
Gaelic, meaning 'dark-haired' or 'dark-skinned'.

Keith
Gaelic, meaning 'woodland'.

Kekoa
Hawaiian, meaning 'brave one' or 'soldier'.

Kelby
Old English, meaning 'farmhouse near the stream'.

Kell
(alt. Kellan, Kellen, Kelley, Kelly, Kiel)
Norse, meaning 'spring'.

Kelsey
Old English, meaning 'victorious ship'.

Kelton
Old English, meaning 'town of the keels'.

Kelvin
Old English, meaning 'friend of ships'.

Ken
Shortened form of Kenneth, meaning 'born of fire'.

Kendal
Old English, meaning 'the Kent river valley'.

Kendon
Old English, meaning 'brave guard'.

Kendrick
Gaelic, meaning 'royal ruler'.

Kenelm
Old English, meaning 'bold'.

Kenji
Japanese, meaning 'intelligent second son'.

Kennedy
Gaelic, meaning 'helmet head'.

Kenneth
(alt. Kenney)
Gaelic, meaning 'born of fire'.

Kennison
English, meaning 'son of Kenneth'.

Kent
From the English county.

Kenton
English, meaning 'town of Ken'.

Kenya
(alt. Kenyon)
From the country in Africa.

Kenyatta
From Kenya.

Kenzo
Japanese, meaning 'wise'.

Keola
Hawaiian, meaning 'life'.

Keon
(alt. Keoni)
Hawaiian, meaning 'gracious'.

Kepler
German, meaning 'hat maker'.

Kermit
(alt. Kerwin)
Gaelic, meaning 'without envy'. Associated with Kermit the Frog.

Kerr
English, meaning 'wetland'.

Keshav
Indian, meaning 'beautiful-haired'.

Kevin
Gaelic, meaning 'handsome beloved'.

Khalid
(alt. Khalif, Khalil)
Arabic, meaning 'immortal'.

Kian
(alt. Keyon, Kyan)
Irish, meaning 'ancient'.

Kiefer
German, meaning 'barrel maker'.

Kieran
(alt. Kieron, Kyron)
Gaelic, meaning 'black'.

Kijana
African, meaning 'youth'.

Kilby
English, from the town of the same name.

Kilian
Irish, meaning 'bright-headed'.

Kimani
African, meaning 'beautiful and sweet'.

King
English, from the word 'king'.

Kingsley
English, meaning 'the king's meadow'.

Kirby
German, meaning 'settlement by a church'.

Kirk
Old German, meaning 'church'.

Klaus
German, meaning 'victorious'.

Kobe
(alt. Koda, Kody)
Japanese, meaning 'a Japanese city'.

Kofi
Ghanaian, meaning 'born on Friday'.

Kohana
Japanese, meaning 'little flower'.

Kojo
Ghanaian, meaning 'Monday'.

Kolby
Norse, meaning 'settlement'.

Korbin
Gaelic, meaning 'a steep hill'.

Kramer
German, meaning 'shopkeeper'.

Kris
(alt. Krish)
From Christopher, meaning 'bearing Christ inside'.

Kurt
German, meaning 'courageous advice'.

Kurtis
French, meaning 'courtier'.

Kwame
Ghanaian, meaning 'born on Saturday'.

Kyden
English, meaning 'narrow little fire'.

Kylan
(alt. Kyle, Kyleb, Kyler)
Gaelic, meaning 'narrow and straight'.

Kyllion
Irish, meaning 'war'.

Kyree
From Cree, a Canadian tribe.

Kyros
Greek, meaning 'legitimate power'.

K

Famous male guitarists

Brian (May)
Carlos (Santana)
Chuck (Berry)
Eddie (Van Halen)
Eric (Clapton)
Frank (Zappa)
Jeff (Beck)
Jimi/Jimmy (Hendrix/Page)
Joe (Satriani)
Keith (Richards)
Prince (Rogers Nelson)

L

Boys' names

Laban
Hebrew, meaning 'white'.

Lachlan
Gaelic, meaning 'from the land of lakes'.

Lacy
Old French, after the place in France.

Lalit
Hindi, meaning 'beautiful'.

Lamar
Old German, meaning 'water'.

Lambert
Scandinavian, meaning 'land brilliant'.

Lambros
Greek, meaning 'brilliant and radiant'.

Lamont
Old Norse, meaning 'law man'.

Lance
French, meaning 'land'.

Lancelot
Variant of Lance, meaning 'land'. The name of one of the Knights of the Round Table.

Landen
(alt. Lando, Landon, Landyn, Langdon)
English, meaning 'long hill'.

Lane
(alt. Layne)
English, from the word 'lanel'.

Lannie
(alt. Lanny)
German, meaning 'precious'.

L

Larkin
Gaelic, meaning 'rough' or 'fierce'.

Laron
French, meaning 'thief'.

Larry
Shortened form of Lawrence, meaning 'man from Laurentum'.

Lars
Scandinavian variant of Lawrence, meaning 'man from Laurentum'.

Lasse
Finnish, meaning 'girl'. (Still, ironically, a boy's name.)

Laszlo
Hungarian, meaning 'glorious rule'.

Lathyn
Latin, meaning 'fighter'.

Latif
Arabic, meaning 'gentle'.

Laurel
Latin, meaning 'bay'.

Laurent
French, from Lawrence, meaning 'man from Laurentum'.

Lawrence
Latin, meaning 'man from Laurentum'.

Lawsan
Old English, meaning 'son of Lawrence'.

Lazarus
Hebrew, meaning 'God is my help'.

Leandro
Latin, meaning 'lion man'.

Lear
German, meaning 'of the meadow'.

Lee
(alt. Leigh)
Old English, meaning 'meadow' or 'valley'.

Leib
German, meaning 'love'.

Leif
Scandinavian, meaning 'heir'.

Leith
From the Scottish town of the same name.

Lennox
(alt. Lenny)
Gaelic, meaning 'with many elm trees'.

L

Leo
Latin, meaning 'lion'.

Leon
Latin, meaning 'lion'.

Leonard
Old German, meaning 'lion strength'.

Leonardo
Italian, meaning 'bold lion'. Artist Leonardo da Vinci painted the hugely famous Mona Lisa.

Leopold
German, meaning 'brave people'.

Leroy
French, meaning 'king'.

Lesley
(alt. Les)
Scottish, meaning 'holly garden'.

Lester
English, meaning 'from Leicester'.

Lewis
French, meaning 'renowned fighter'.

Lexar
(alt. Lexer)
Shortened form of Alexander, meaning 'man's defender'.

Liam
German, meaning 'helmet'.

Lincoln
English, meaning 'lake colony'.

Lindsay
Scottish, meaning 'linden tree'.

Linus
Latin, meaning 'lion'.

Lionel
English, meaning 'lion'.

Llewellyn
Welsh, meaning 'like a lion'.

Lloyd
Welsh, meaning 'gray-haired and sacred'.

Logan
Gaelic, meaning 'hollow'.

Lonnie
English, meaning 'lion strength'.

Lorcan
Gaelic, meaning 'little fierce one'.

Louis
(alt. Lou, Louie, Luigi, Luis)
German, meaning 'famous warrior'.

143

L

Lucas
(alt. Lukas, Luca)
English, meaning 'man from Luciana'.

Lucian
(alt. Lucio)
Latin, meaning 'light'.

Ludwig
German, meaning 'famous fighter'.

Luke
(alt. Luc, Luka)
Latin, meaning 'from Lucanus' (in southern Italy).

Lupe
Latin, meaning 'wolf'.

Luther
German, meaning 'soldier of the people'. Superman's arch enemy is supervillain Lex Luther.

Lyle
French, meaning 'the island'.

Lyn
(alt. Lyndon)
Spanish, meaning 'pretty'.

M Boys' names

Mac
(alt. Mack, Mackie)
Scottish, meaning 'son of'.

Macaulay
Scottish, meaning 'son of the phantom'. Made famous by child actor Macaulay Culkin.

Mace
English, meaning 'heavy staff' or 'club'.

Mackenzie
Scottish, meaning 'the fair one'.

Mackland
Scottish, meaning 'land of Mac'.

Macon
French, from the name of towns in France and Georgia.

Macsen
Scottish, meaning 'son of Mac'.

Madden
(alt. Mads)
Irish, meaning 'descendant of the hound'.

Maddox
(alt. Maddux)
English, meaning 'good' or 'generous'.

Madison
(alt. Madsen)
Irish, meaning 'son of Madden'.

Magnus
(alt. Manus)
Latin, meaning 'great'.

Maguire
Gaelic, meaning 'son of the beige one'.

M

Mahesh
Hindi, meaning 'great ruler'.

Mahir
Arabic, meaning 'skillful'.

Mahlon
Hebrew, meaning 'sickness'.

Mahmoud
Arabic, meaning 'praise-worthy'.

Mahoney
Irish, meaning 'bear'.

Major
English, from the word 'major'. One of the fastest climbing boys' names in 2013.

Makal
From Michael, meaning 'close to God'.

Makani
Hawaiian, meaning 'wind'.

Makis
Hebrew, meaning 'gift from God'.

Mako
Hebrew, meaning 'God is with us'.

Malachi
(alt. Malachy)
Irish, meaning 'messenger of God'.

Malcolm
English, meaning 'Columba's servant'.

Mali
Arabic, meaning 'full and rich'.

Manfred
Old German, meaning 'man of peace'.

Manish
English, meaning 'manly'.

Manley
English, meaning 'manly and brave'.

Mannix
Gaelic, meaning 'little monk'.

Manoi
(alt. Manos)
Japanese, meaning 'love springing from intellect'.

Manuel
Hebrew, meaning 'God is with us'.

Manzi
Italian, meaning 'steer'.

Marc
(alt. Marco, Marcos, Marcus, Markel)
French, meaning 'from the god Mars'.

Marcel
(alt. Marcelino, Marcello)
French, meaning 'little warrior'.

Marek
Polish variant of Mark, meaning 'from the god Mars'.

Mariano
Latin, meaning 'from the god Mars'.

Mario
(alt. Marius)
Latin, meaning 'manly'.

Mark
(alt. Markus)
English, meaning 'from the god Mars'.

Marley
(alt. Marlin, Marlow)
Old English, meaning 'meadow near the lake'.

Marlon
English origin, meaning 'little hawk'. Made famous by actor Marlon Brando.

Marshall
Old French, meaning 'caretaker of horses'.

Martin
(alt. Marty)
Latin, meaning 'dedicated to Mars'.

Marvel
English, from the word 'marvel'.

Marvin
Welsh, meaning 'sea friend'.

Mason
English, from the word mason.

Mathias
(alt. Matthias)
Hebrew, meaning 'gift of God'.

Matthew
(alt. Mathieu)
Hebrew, meaning 'gift of the Lord'.

Maurice
(alt. Mauricio)
Latin, meaning 'dark skinned' or 'Moorish'.

Maverick
American, meaning 'non-conformist leader'. Made popular by the movie *Top Gun*.

Max
(alt. Maxie, Maxim)
Latin, meaning 'greatest'.

Maximillian
Latin, meaning 'greatest'.

Maximino
Latin, meaning 'little Max'.

M

Maxwell
Latin, meaning 'Maccus' stream'.

Maynard
Old German, meaning 'brave'.

McArthur
Scottish, meaning 'son of Arthur'.

McCoy
Scottish, meaning 'son of Coy'.

Mearl
English, meaning 'my earl'.

Mederic
French, meaning 'doctor'.

Mekhi
African, meaning 'who is God?'. Actor Mekhi Phifer is known for his roles in ER and *8 Mile*.

Mel
Gaelic, meaning 'smooth brow'.

Melbourne
From the city in Australia.

Melchior
Persian, meaning 'king of the city'.

Melton
English, meaning 'town of Mel'.

Melva
Hawaiian, meaning 'plumeria'.

Melville
Scottish, meaning 'town of Mel'.

Melvin
(alt. Melvyn)
English, meaning 'smooth brow'.

Memphis
Greek, meaning 'established and beautiful'.

Mercer
English, from the word 'mercer'.

Merl
French, meaning 'blackbird'.

Merlin
Welsh, meaning 'sea fortress'. Merlin is perhaps the most famous wizard of all, appearing in stories from the medieval era.

Merrick
Welsh, meaning 'Moorish'.

Merrill
Gaelic, meaning 'shining sea'.

Merritt
English, from the word 'merit'.

Merton
Old English, meaning 'town by the lake'.

Meyer
Hebrew, meaning 'bright farmer'.

Michael
(alt. Michel, Michele)
Hebrew, meaning 'resembles God'.

Michalis
(alt. Miklos)
Greek form of Michael, meaning 'resembles God'.

Michelangelo
Italian, meaning 'Michael's angel'. Name of the famous Italian artist who painted the Sistine Chapel.

Miguel
Spanish form of Michael meaning 'resembles God'.

Mike
(alt. Mick, Mickey, Mikie)
Shortened form of Michael meaning 'resembles God'.

Milan
From the name of the Italian city.

Miles
(alt. Milo, Milos, Myles)
English, from the word 'miles'.

Milton
English, meaning 'miller's town'.

Miro
Slavic, meaning 'peace'.

Misha
Russian, meaning 'who is like God'.

Mitch
Shortened form of Mitchell, meaning 'who is like God'.

Mitchell
English, meaning 'who is like God'.

Modesto
Italian, meaning 'modest'.

Moe
Hebrew, meaning 'God's helmet'.

Mohamed
(alt. Mohammad, Mohamet, Mohammed, Muhammad)
Arabic, meaning 'praiseworthy'.

Monroe
Gaelic, meaning 'mouth of the river Rotha'.

Monserrate
Latin, meaning 'jagged mountain'.

M

Football players

Bart (Starr)
Deacon (Jones)
Dick (Butkus)
Donald (Driver)
Emmitt (Smith)
Jacoby (Jones)
Jerry (Rice)
Jim (Brown)
Joe (Namath/Montana)
John/Johnny (Elway/ Unitas)

Montague
French, meaning 'pointed hill'.

Montana
Latin, meaning 'mountain'.

Monte
Italian, meaning 'mountain'.

Montgomery
Variant of Montague, meaning 'pointed hill'.

Monty
Shortened form of Montague, meaning 'pointed hill'.

Moody
English, from the word 'moody'.

Mordecai
Hebrew, meaning 'little man'.

Morgan
Welsh, meaning 'circling sea'.

Moritz
Latin, meaning 'dark skinned and Moorish'.

Morpheus
Greek, meaning 'shape'.

Morris
Welsh, meaning 'dark-skinned and Moorish'.

Morrison
English, meaning 'son of Morris'.

Moroccan
Arabic, meaning 'from Morocco'.

Mortimer
French, meaning 'dead sea'.

Morton
Old English, meaning 'moor town'.

Moses
(alt. Moshe, Moshon)
Hebrew, meaning 'savior'. A key biblical figure.

Moss
English, from the word 'moss'.

Mungo
Gaelic, meaning 'most dear'.

Murl
French, meaning 'blackbird'.

Murphy
Irish, meaning 'sea warrior'.

Murray
Gaelic, meaning 'lord and master'.

Mustafa
Arabic, meaning 'chosen'.

Myron
Greek, meaning 'myrrh'.

M

N Boys' names

Najee
Arabic, meaning 'dear companion'.

Nakia
Arabic, meaning 'pure'.

Nakul
Indian, meaning 'mongoose'.

Naphtali
Hebrew, meaning 'wrestling'.

Napoleon
Italian origin, meaning 'man from Naples'. Name of the French general who became Emperor of France.

Narciso
Latin, from the myth of Narcissus, who was famous for drowning after gazing at his own reflection.

Nash
English, meaning 'at the ash tree'.

Nasir
Arabic, meaning 'helper'.

Nate
Hebrew, meaning 'God has given'.

Nathan
(alt. Nathaniel)
Hebrew, meaning 'God has given'.

Naveen
Indian, meaning 'new'.

Neal
Irish, meaning 'champion'.

Ned
Nickname for Edward, meaning 'wealthy guard'.

N

Popular song names

Alexander ("Alexander's Ragtime Band", Irving Berlin)
Daniel ("Daniel", Elton John)
Frankie ("Frankie", Sister Sledge)
Jack ("Jumpin' Jack Flash", The Rolling Stones)
James ("James Dean", The Eagles)
Johnny ("Johnny B. Goode", Chuck Berry)
Kenneth ("What's the Frequency, Kenneth?", REM)
Leroy ("Bad, Bad Leroy Brown", Jim Croce)
Mack ("Mack The Knife", Bobby Darin)
Oliver ("Oliver's Army", Elvis Costello)

Neftali
Hebrew, meaning 'struggling'.

Nehemiah
Hebrew, meaning 'comforter'.

Neil
(alt. Niall)
Irish, meaning 'champion'.

Neilson
Irish, meaning 'son of Neil'.

Nelson
Variant of Neil, meaning
'champion'

Nemo
Latin, meaning 'nobody'. Made
popular after the Disney/Pixar
film *Finding Nemo*.

Neo
Latin, meaning 'new'.

Nephi
Greek, meaning 'cloud'.

Nessim
Arabic, meaning 'breeze'.

Nestor
Greek, meaning 'traveller'.

Neville
Old French, meaning 'new
village'.

Newton
English, meaning 'new town'.

Nicholas
(alt. Nick, Nicklas, Nico, Niklas)
Greek, meaning 'victorious'.

N

Nigel
Gaelic, meaning 'champion'.

Nikhil
Hindi, meaning 'whole' or 'entire'.

Nikita
Greek, meaning 'unconquered'. Also a girls' name.

Nikolai
(alt. Niko, Nikos)
Russian variant of Nicholas, meaning 'victorious'.

Nimrod
Hebrew, meaning 'we will rebel'.

Nissim
Hebrew, meaning 'wonderful things'.

Noah
Hebrew, meaning 'peaceful'. A key biblical figure.

Noel
French, meaning 'Christmas'.

Nolan
Gaelic, meaning 'champion'.

Norbert
Old German, meaning 'northern brightness'.

Norman
Old German, meaning 'northerner'.

Normand
French, meaning 'from Normandy'.

Norris
Old French, meaning 'northerner'.

Norton
English, meaning 'northern town'.

Norval
French, meaning 'northern town'.

Names of gods

Anubis (Death: Egyptian)
Apollo (Sun: Roman)
Brahma (Creation: Hindu)
Eros (Love: Greek)
Hypnos (Sleep: Greek)
Mars (War: Roman)
Neptune (Sea: Roman)
Ra (Sun: Egyptian)
Shiva (Destruction: Hindu)
Vishnu (Preservation: Hindu)

N

Norwood
English, meaning 'Northern forest'.

Nova
Latin, meaning 'new'.

Nuno
Latin, meaning 'ninth'.

Nunzio
Italian, meaning 'messenger'.

O

Boys' names

Oakley
English, meaning 'from the oak meadow'.

Obadiah
Hebrew, meaning 'God's worker'.

Obama
African, meaning 'crooked'. Last name of the current President of the United States.

Obed
Hebrew, meaning 'servant of God'.

Oberon
Old German, meaning 'royal bear'.

Obie
Shortened form of Oberon, meaning 'royal bear'.

Spelling options

A vs E (Aiden or Aidan)
F vs PH (Josef or Joseph)
I vs Y (Henri or Henry)
IE vs Y (Donnie or Donny)
J vs G (Jorge or George)
N vs HN (Jon or John)
QUE vs CK (Frederique or Frederick)

O

Octave
(alt. Octavian, Octavio)
Latin, meaning 'eight'.

Oda
(alt. Odell, Odie, Odis)
Hebrew, meaning 'praise God'.

Ogden
Old English, meaning 'oak valley'.

Oisin
From the Irish poet.

Ola
Norse, meaning 'precious'.

Olaf
(alt. Olan)
Old Norse, meaning 'ancestor'.

Oleander
Hawaiian, meaning 'joyous'.

Oleg
(alt. Olen)
Russian, meaning 'holy'.

Olin
Russian, meaning 'rock'.

Oliver
(alt. Olivier, Ollie, Olly)
Latin, meaning 'olive tree'.

Omar
(alt. Omari, Omarion)
Arabic, meaning 'speaker'.

Ora
Latin, meaning 'hour'.

Oran
(alt. Oren, Orrin)
Gaelic, meaning 'light and pale'.

Orange
English, from the word 'orange'.

Orion
From the Greek hunter.

Orlando
(alt. Orlo)
Old German, meaning 'old land'.

Orpheus
Greek, meaning 'beautiful voice'. A legendary Greek musician, poet and prophet.

Orson
Latin, meaning 'bear'.

Orville
Old French, meaning 'gold town'.

Osaka
From the Japanese city.

Osborne
Norse, meaning 'bear god'.

Oscar
Old English, meaning 'spear of the gods'.

O

Oswald
German, meaning 'God's power'.

Otha
(alt. Otho)
German, meaning 'wealth'.

Othello
Old German, meaning 'wealth'. From the Shakespearean character and play.

Otis
German, meaning 'wealth'.

Otten
English, meaning 'otter-like'.

Otto
Italian, meaning 'eight'.

Owain
Welsh, meaning 'youth'.

Owen
Welsh, meaning 'well born and noble'.

Oz
Hebrew, meaning 'strength'.

Popular Asian names for boys and girls

Bao
Cái
Huang
Jiro
Kei
Ming
Miyoko
Shen
Tai
Yoko

P Boys' names

Pablo
Spanish, meaning 'little'.

Paddy
Shortened form of Patrick, meaning 'noble'.

Padma
Sanskrit, meaning 'lotus'.

Padraig
Irish, meaning 'noble'.

Panos
Greek, meaning 'all holy'.

Paolo
Italian, meaning 'little'.

Paresh
Indian, meaning 'supreme standard'.

Parker
Old English, meaning 'park keeper'.

Pascal
Latin, meaning 'Easter child'.

Patrick
(alt. Pat, Patrice)
Irish, meaning 'noble'.

Patten
English, meaning 'noble'.

Paul
Hebrew, meaning 'small'. Paul was one of Jesus' main disciples.

Pavel
Latin, meaning 'small'.

Pax
Latin, meaning 'peace'.

Paxton
English, meaning 'town of peace'.

Payne
Latin, meaning 'peasant'.

P

Payton
Latin, meaning 'peasant's town'.

Pedro
Spanish form of Peter, meaning 'rock'.

Penn
English, meaning 'hill'. Penn & Teller are a comedy magician/ entertainment duo.

Percival
(alt. Percy)
French, meaning 'pierce the valley'.

Perez
Hebrew, meaning 'breach'.

Pericles
Greek, meaning 'far-famed'.

Perrin
Greek, meaning 'rock'.

Perry
English, meaning 'rock'.

Pervis
English, meaning 'purveyor'.

Peter
(alt. Pete, Petros)
Greek, meaning 'rock'.

Peyton
Old English, meaning 'fighting man's estate'.

Philip
(alt. Phil)
Greek, meaning 'lover of horses'.

Philo
Greek, meaning 'love'.

Phineas
(alt. Pinchas)
Hebrew, meaning 'oracle'.

Phoenix
Greek, meaning 'dark red'.

Pierre
French form of Peter, meaning 'rock'.

Piers
Greek form of Peter, meaning 'rock'.

No-nickname names

Alex
Jude
Keith
Otto
Owen
Toby

162

P

Pierson
Variant of Pierce, meaning 'son of Piers'.

Pip
Greek, meaning 'lover of horses'.

Placido
Latin, meaning 'placid'.

Pradeep
Hindi, meaning 'light'.

Pranav
Hindi, meaning 'spiritual leader'.

Presley
Old English, meaning 'priest's meadow'.

Preston
Old English, meaning 'priest's town'.

Primo
Italian, meaning 'first'.

Primus
Latin, meaning 'first'.

Prince
English, from the word 'prince'. Made popular after singer and guitarist Prince.

Prospero
Latin, meaning 'prosperous'.

Pryce
(alt. Prize)
Old French, meaning 'prize'.

Pryor
English, meaning 'first'.

Ptolemy
Greek, meaning 'aggressive' or 'warlike'.

Foreign alternatives

David (Dafydd, Dann)
John (Jean, Juan)
Joseph (Giuseppe, José)
Michael (Miguel, Mikhail)
Owen (Eoghan, Owain)
Peter (Pedro, Pierre, Pieter)
Richard (Ricardo)

Boys' names

Quabil
(alt. Quadim)
Arabic, meaning 'able'.

Quadir
Arabic, meaning 'powerful'.

Quaid
Irish, meaning 'fourth'. Made popular after actor Dennis Quaid.

Quemby
Norse, meaning 'from the woman's estate'.

Quentin
(alt. Quinten, Quintin, Quinton, Quintus)
Latin, meaning 'fifth'.

Quillan
Gaelic, meaning 'sword'.

Quillon
Gaelic, meaning 'club'.

Quincy
Old French, meaning 'estate of the fifth son'.

Quinlan
Gaelic, meaning 'fit, shapely and strong'.

Quinn
Gaelic, meaning 'counsel'.

'Powerful' names

Americo	Michio
Daivat	Oswald
Derek	Oz
Hercules	Roderick
Kano	Thor

R Boys' names

Radames
Slavic, meaning 'famous joy'.

Raekwon
Hebrew, meaning 'God has healed'.

Rafael
(alt. Rafe, Rafer, Raffi, Raphael)
Hebrew, meaning 'God has healed'.

Ragnar
Old Norse, meaning 'judgement warrior'. Ragnar Lodbrok was a legendary Norse ruler from the Viking Era.

Raheem
Arabic, meaning 'merciful and kind'.

Rahm
Hebrew, meaning 'pleasing'.

Rahul
(alt. Raoul, Raul)
Indian, meaning 'efficient'.

Raiden
(alt. Rainen)
From the Japanese god of thunder.

Rainen
Old German, meaning 'deciding warrior'.

Raj
Indian, meaning 'king'.

Rajesh
(alt. Ramesh)
Indian, meaning 'ruler of kings'.

Raleigh
Old English, meaning 'deer's meadow'.

R

Ralph
Old English, meaning 'wolf'.

Ram
English, from the word 'ram'.

Ramiro
Germanic, meaning 'powerful in battle'.

Ramsey
(alt. Ramsay)
Old English, meaning 'wild garlic island'. Currently associated with chef Gordon Ramsey.

Randall
(alt. Randolph, Randy)
Old German, meaning 'wolf shield'.

Raniel
English, meaning 'God is my happiness'.

Ranjit
Indian, meaning 'influenced by charm'.

Rannoch
Gaelic, meaning 'fern'.

Rashad
Arabic, meaning 'good judgment'.

Rasheed
(alt. Rashid)
Indian, meaning 'rightly guided'.

Rasmus
Greek, meaning 'beloved'.

Raven
English, from the word 'raven'.

Ravi
French, meaning 'delighted'.

Ray
English, from the word 'ray'.

Raymond
(alt. Rayner)
English, meaning 'advisor'.

Raz
Israeli, meaning 'secret' or 'mystery'.

Reagan
Irish, meaning 'little king'. Ronald Reagan was the 40th President of the United States.

Reggie
Latin, meaning 'queen'.

Reginald
(alt. Ren)
Latin, meaning 'regal'.

Regis
Shortened form of Reginald, meaning 'regal'.

R

Reid
Old English, meaning 'by the reeds'.

Reilly
(alt. Riley)
English, meaning 'courageous'.

Remus
Latin, meaning 'swift'.

Rémy
French, meaning 'from Rheims'.

Renato
Latin, meaning 'rebirth'.

Rene
French, meaning 'rebirth'.

Reno
Latin, meaning 'renewed'. Also the name of the city in Nevada.

Reuben
Spanish, meaning 'a son'.

Reuel
Hebrew, meaning 'friend of God'.

Rex
Latin, meaning 'king'.

Rey
Spanish, meaning 'king'.

Reynold
Latin, meaning 'king's advisor'.

Rhodes
German, meaning 'where the roses grow'. Also the name of the Greek island.

Rhodri
Welsh, meaning 'ruler of the circle'.

Rhys
(alt. Reece, Riece)
Welsh, meaning 'enthusiasm'.

Richard
(alt. Ricardo, Richie, Rick, Ricki, Ricky, Rikardo, Ritchie)
Old German, meaning 'powerful leader'.

Ridley
English, meaning 'cleared wood'.

Rigby
English, from the place in Lancashire.

Riky
Irish Gaelic, meaning 'courageous'.

Ringo
English, meaning 'ring'. Associated with drummer Ringo Starr from The Beatles.

R

Rio
Spanish, meaning 'river'.

Riordan
Gaelic, meaning 'bard'.

Rishi
Variant of Richard, meaning 'powerful leader'.

Roald
Scandinavian, meaning 'ruler'.

Robert
(alt. Rob, Robbie, Roberto)
Old German, meaning 'bright fame'.

Robin
English, from the word 'robin'.

Robinson
English, meaning 'son of Robin'.

Rocco
(alt. Rocky)
Italian, meaning 'rest'.

Roderick
German, meaning 'famous power'.

Rodney
(alt. Rod, Roddy)
Old German, meaning 'island near the clearing'.

Rodrigo
Spanish form of Roderick, meaning 'famous power'.

Roger
Old German, meaning 'spear man'.

Roland
Old German, meaning 'renowned land'.

Rolf
Old German, meaning 'wolf'.

Rollie
(alt. Rollo)
Old German, meaning 'renowned land'.

Roman
Latin, meaning 'from Rome'.

Romeo
Latin, meaning 'pilgrim to Rome'. Made famous by Shakespeare's play.

Ronald
(alt. Ron, Ronnie)
Norse, meaning 'mountain of strength'.

Ronan
Gaelic, meaning 'little seal'.

Rory
English, meaning 'red king'.

R

Ross
(alt. Russ)
Scottish, meaning 'cape'.

Rowan
(alt. Roan)
Gaelic, meaning 'little red one'.
Also refers to the rowan tree.

Roy
Gaelic, meaning 'red'.

Ruben
Hebrew, meaning 'son'.

Rudolph
(alt. Rudy)
Old German, meaning
'famous wolf'.

Rufus
Latin, meaning 'red-haired'.

Rupert
Variant of Robert, meaning
'bright fame'.

Russell
Old French, meaning 'little
red one'.

Rusty
English, meaning 'ruddy'.

Ryan
Gaelic, meaning 'little king'.

Ryder
English, meaning 'horseman'.

Rye
English, from the word 'rye'.

Ryker
From Richard, meaning
'powerful leader'. *Ryker's
Islands* is a fictional prison
facility in Marvel Comics
stories.

Rylan
English, meaning 'land where
rye is grown'.

Ryley
Old English, meaning 'rye
clearing'.

S Boys' names

Saber
French, meaning 'sword'.

Sagar
African, meaning 'ruler of the water'.

Sage
English, meaning 'wise'.

Sakari
Native American, meaning 'sweet'.

Salim
Arabic, meaning 'secure'.

Salvador
Spanish, meaning 'savior'.

Salvatore
Italian, meaning 'savior'.

Samir
Arabic, meaning 'pleasant companion'.

Samson
Hebrew, meaning 'son of Sam'.

Spring names

Alvern
Attwell
Avir
Bradwell
Jarek
Kell
Marcus
Rain
Tamiko
Weldon

S

Samuel
(alt. Sam, Sama, Sammie, Sammy)
Hebrew, meaning 'God is heard'.

Sandeep
Indian, meaning 'lighting the way'.

Sandro
Shortened form of Alessandro, meaning 'defending men'.

Sandy
Shortened form of Alexander, meaning 'defending men'.

Sanjay
Indian, meaning 'victory'.

Santana
Spanish, meaning 'saint'. Made famous by guitarist Carlos Santana.

Santiago
Spanish, meaning 'Saint James'.

Santino
Spanish, meaning 'little Saint James'.

Santo
(alt. Santos)
Latin, meaning 'saint'.

Sascha
(alt. Sacha, Sasha)
Shortened Russian form of Alexander, meaning 'defending men'.

Sawyer
English, meaning 'one who saws wood'.

Scott
(alt. Scottie)
English, meaning 'from Scotland'.

Seamus
Irish variant of James, meaning 'he who supplants'.

Sean
(alt. Shaun)
Variant of John, meaning 'God is gracious'.

Sebastian
Greek, meaning 'revered'.

Sébastien
French form of Sebastian, meaning 'revered'.

Sergio
Latin, meaning 'servant'.

Seth
Hebrew, meaning 'appointed'.

Severus
Latin, meaning 'severe'.

S

Seymour
English, from the place name in northern France.

Shane
Variant of Sean, meaning 'God is gracious'.

Sharif
Arabic, meaning 'honored'.

Shea
Gaelic, meaning 'admirable'.

Shelby
Norse, meaning 'willow'.

Sherlock
English, meaning 'fair-haired'. The name of the lead character in Sir Arthur Conan Doyle's *Sherlock Holmes* novels.

Sherman
Old English, meaning 'shear man'.

Shmuel
Hebrew, meaning 'his name is God'.

Shola
Arabic, meaning 'energetic'.

Sidney
(alt. Sid, Sydney)
English, meaning 'wide meadow'.

Sigmund
Old German, meaning 'victorious hand'.

Silvanus
(alt. Silvio)
Latin, meaning 'woods'.

Simba
(alt. Sim)
Swahili, meaning 'lion'.

Simon
(alt. Simeon)
Hebrew, meaning 'to hear'.

Sinbad
Literary merchant adventurer.

Sindri
Norse, meaning 'dwarf'.

Summer names

Augustus
Balder
Cain
Dax
Leo
Sky
Somers
Sunny
Theros

S

Sipho
African, meaning 'the unknown one'.

Sire
English, from the word 'sire'.

Sirius
Hebrew, meaning 'brightest star'.

Skipper
English, meaning 'ship captain'.

Skyler
Dutch, meaning 'guarded' or 'scholar'.

Solomon
Hebrew, meaning 'peace'.

Sonny
American English, meaning 'son'. A term of endearment in western cultures.

Soren
Scandinavian, meaning 'brightest star'.

Spencer
English, meaning 'dispenser'.

Spike
English, from the word 'spike'.

Stanford
English, meaning 'stone ford'.

Stanley
(alt. Stan)
English, meaning 'stony meadow'.

Stavros
Greek, meaning 'crowned'.

Stellan
Latin, meaning 'starred'.

Steno
German, meaning 'stone'.

Stephen
(alt. Stefan, Stefano, Steffan, Steve, Steven, Stevie)
English, meaning 'crowned'.

Stoney
English, meaning 'stone like'.

Fall names

Aki
Akiko
Demitrius
Dionysus
Forrest
George
Goren
Hunter
Red
Storm

S

Storm
English, from the word 'storm'. Storm is a key (female) character in the *X-men* comic book series.

Stuart
(alt. Stewart)
English, meaning 'steward'.

Sven
Norse, meaning 'boy'.

Syed
Arabic, meaning 'lucky'.

Sylvester
Latin, meaning 'wooded'.

Popular Australian names for boys and girls

Adelaide	Hobart
Brad	Lorrae
Darwin	Narelle
Evonne	Raelene
Griffith	Tallara

T

Boys' names

Tacitus
Latin, meaning 'silent, calm'. Also the name of a Roman historian.

Tad
English, from the word 'tadpole'.

Taj
Indian, meaning 'crown'.

Takashi
Japanese, meaning 'praiseworthy'.

Takoda
Sioux, meaning 'friend to everyone'.

Talbot
(alt. Tal)
Aristocratic English name.

Tamir
Arabic, meaning 'tall and wealthy'.

Tanner
Old English, meaning 'leather-maker'.

Taras
(alt. Tarez)
Scottish, meaning 'crag'.

Tarek
Arabic, meaning 'evening caller'.

Tarian
Welsh, meaning 'silver'.

Tariq
Arabic, meaning 'morning star'.

Tarquin
Latin, from the Roman clan name.

179

T

Tarun
Hindi, meaning 'young'.

Tatanka
Hebrew, meaning 'bull'.

Tate
English, meaning 'cheerful'.

Taurean
English, meaning 'bull-like'.

Tavares
English, meaning 'descendant of the hermit'.

Tave
(alt. Tavian, Tavis, Tavish)
French, from Gustave, meaning 'royal staff'.

Taylor
(alt. Tay)
English, meaning 'tailor'.

Ted
(alt. Teddy)
English, from Edward, meaning 'wealthy guard'.

Tennessee
Native American, meaning 'river town'.

Terence
(alt. Terrill, Terry)
English, meaning 'tender'.

Tex
English, meaning 'Texan'.

Thane
(alt. Thayer)
Scottish, meaning 'landholder'.

Thatcher
(alt. Thaxter)
Old English, meaning 'roof thatcher'. Associated with former British Prime Minister Margaret Thatcher.

Thelonius
Latin, meaning 'ruler of the people'.

Theodore
(alt. Theo)
Greek, meaning 'God's gift'.

Theophile
Latin, meaning 'God's love'.

Theron
Greek, meaning 'hunter'.

Thierry
French variant of Terence, meaning 'tender'.

Thomas
(alt. Thom, Tom, Tomlin, Tommy)
Aramaic, meaning 'twin'.

Thomsen
(alt. Thomson)
English, meaning 'son of Thomas'.

T

Thor
Norse, meaning 'thunder'.
Thor was a hammer-wielding
deity in Norse mythology.

Tiago
From Santiago, meaning 'Saint
James'.

Tiberius
English, meaning 'from the river
Tiber'.

Tibor
Latin, from the river Tiber.

Tiernan
Gaelic, meaning 'lord'.

Tilden
(alt. Till)
English, meaning 'fertile valley'.

Timothy
(alt. Tim, Timmie, Timmy, Timon)
Greek, meaning 'God's honor'.

Tito
(alt. Titus, Tizian)
Latin, meaning 'defender'.

Tobias
(alt. Toby)
Hebrew, meaning 'God is
good'.

Tod
(alt. Todd)
English, meaning 'fox'.

Tonneau
French, meaning 'barrel'.

Tony
Shortened form of Anthony,
from the old Roman family
name.

Torey
Norse, meaning 'Thor'.

Torin
Gaelic, meaning 'chief'.

Torquil
Gaelic, meaning 'helmet'.

Toshi
Japanese, meaning 'reflection'.

Travis
French, meaning 'crossover'.

Trevor
(alt. Tvevin)
Welsh origin, meaning 'great
settlement'.

Trey
(alt. Tyree)
French, meaning 'very'.

Tristan
(alt. Tristram)
Celtic from the Celtic hero.

Troy
Gaelic, meaning 'descended
from the soldier'.

T

Tudor
Variant of Theodore, meaning 'God's gift'. Also the British dynasty, which ruled between 1485–1603.

Tyler
English, meaning 'tile maker'.

Tyrell
French, meaning 'puller'.

Tyrone
Gaelic, meaning 'Owen's county'.

Tyson
English, meaning 'son of Tyrone'.

Winter names

Aquilo
Caldwell
Colden
Crispin
Darke
Eirwen
Gennaio
Jack
Mistral
Rain

U

Boys' names

Uberto
(alt. Umberto)
Italian, variant of Hubert,
meaning 'bright or shining
intellect'.

Udo
German, meaning 'power of
the wolf'.

Ugo
Italian form of Hugo, meaning
'mind and heart'.

Ulf
German, meaning 'wolf'.

Ulrich
German, meaning 'noble ruler'.

Ultan
Irish, meaning 'from Ulster'.

Ulysses
Greek, meaning 'wrathful'.
Made famous by the
mythological voyager.

Upton
English, meaning 'high town'.

Urho
Finnish, meaning 'brave'.

Uri
(alt. Uriah, Urias)
Hebrew, meaning 'my light'.

Uriel
Hebrew, meaning 'angel of
light'.

Usher
English, from the word 'usher'.
Made famous by the R&B star.

U

Uzi
Hebrew, meaning 'my strength'.

Uzzi
(alt. Uzziah)
Hebrew, meaning 'my power'.

Christmas names

Casper
Celyn
Christian
Gabriel
Jesus
Joseph
Nicholas
Noel
Robin

V

Boys' names

Vadim
Russian, meaning 'scandal maker'.

Valdemar
German, meaning 'renowned leader'.

Valente
Latin, meaning 'valiant'.

Valentine
(alt. Val, Valentin, Valentino)
English, from the word 'valentine'. St Valentine's Day is named after Valentinus, who was said to have healed the broken heart of his jailer's daughter.

Valerio
Italian, meaning 'valiant'.

Van
Dutch, meaning 'son of'.

Vance
English, meaning 'marshland'.

Vangelis
Greek, meaning 'good news'.

Varro
Latin, meaning 'strong'.

Varun
Hindi, meaning 'water god'.

Vasilis
Greek, meaning 'kingly'.

Vaughan
Welsh, meaning 'little'.

Vernell
French, meaning 'green and flourishing'.

Verner
German, meaning 'army defender'.

Vernon
(alt. Vernie)
French, meaning 'alder grove'.

Versilius
Latin, meaning 'flier'.

Vester
Latin, meaning 'wooded'.

Victor
(alt. Vic)
Latin, meaning 'champion'.

Vidal
(alt. Vidar)
Spanish, meaning 'life-giving'.

Vijay
Hindi, meaning 'conquering'.

Vikram
Hindi, meaning 'sun'.

Viktor
Latin, meaning 'victory'.

Ville
French, meaning 'town'.

Vincent
(alt. Vince)
English, meaning 'victorious'.

Virgil
Latin, meaning 'staff bearer'.
From the Latin poet.

Vito
Spanish, meaning 'life'.

Vittorio
Italian, meaning 'victory'.

Vitus
Latin, meaning 'life'.

Vivian
Latin, meaning 'lively'.

Vladimir
Slavic, meaning 'prince'.

Volker
German, meaning 'defender of the people'.

Von
Norse, meaning 'hope'.

Boys' names

Wade
English, meaning 'to move forward' or 'to go'.

Waldemar
German, meaning 'famous ruler'.

Walden
English, meaning 'valley of the Britons'.

Waldo
Old German, meaning 'rule'. Ralph Waldo Emerson was a highly influential 19th century essayist and speaker.

Walker
English, meaning 'a fuller'.

Wallace
English, meaning 'foreigner' or 'stranger'.

Wally
German, meaning 'ruler of the army'.

Walter
(alt. Walt)
German, meaning 'ruler of the army'.

Ward
English, meaning 'guardian'.

Wardell
Old English, meaning 'watchman's hill'.

Warner
German, meaning 'army guard'.

Warren
German, meaning 'guard' or 'the game park'.

Warwick
Old English, meaning 'buildings near the weir'. Name of the popular British actor Warwick Davies.

Washington
English, meaning 'clever' or 'clever man's settlement'.

Wassily
Greek, meaning 'royal' or 'kingly'.

Watson
English, meaning 'son' or 'son of Walter'.

Waverley
(alt. Waverly)
English, meaning 'quaking aspen'.

Waylon
English, meaning 'land by the road'.

Wayne
English, meaning 'a cartwright'.

Webster
English, meaning 'weaver'.

Weldon
English, meaning 'from the hill of well' or 'hill with a well'.

Wendell
(alt. Wendel)
German, meaning 'a wend'.

Werner
German, meaning 'army guard'.

Weston
English, meaning 'from the west town'.

Wheeler
English, meaning 'wheel maker'.

Whitley
English, meaning 'white wood'.

Whitman
Old English, meaning 'white man'.

Whitney
Old English, meaning 'white island'.

Wilber
(alt. Wilbur)
Old German, meaning 'bright will'.

Wiley
Old English, meaning 'beguiling' or 'enchanting'.

Wilford
Old English, meaning 'the ford by the willows'.

Wilfredo
(alt. Wilfred, Wilfrid)
English, meaning 'to will peace'.

Wilhelm
(alt. Willem)
German, meaning 'strong-willed warrior'.

Wilkes
(alt. Wilkie)
Old English, meaning 'strong-willed protector' or 'strong and resolute protector'.

William
(alt. Will, Willie, Willy)
English (Teutonic), meaning 'strong protector' or 'strong-willed warrior'.

Willis
English, meaning 'server of William'.

Willoughby
Old Norse and Old English, meaning 'from the farm by the trees'.

Wilmer
English (Teutonic), meaning 'famously resolute'.

Wilmot
English, meaning 'resolute mind'.

Wilson
English, meaning 'son of William'.

Wilton
Old Norse and English, meaning 'from the farm by the brook/streams'.

Windell
(alt. Wendell)
German, meaning 'wanderer' or 'seeker'.

Windsor
Old English, meaning 'river bank' or 'landing place'. The British Royal family is known as the House of Windsor.

Winfield
English, meaning 'from the field of Wina'.

Winslow
Old English, meaning 'victory on the hill'.

Winter
Old English, meaning 'to be born in the winter'.

Winthrop
Old English, meaning 'village of friends'.

Winton
Old English, meaning 'a friend's farm'.

Wirrin
Aboriginal, meaning 'a tea tree'.

Wistan
Old English, meaning 'battle stone' or 'mark of the battle'.

Wittan
Old English, meaning 'farm in the woods' or 'farm by the woods'.

Wolf
(alt. Wolfe)
English, meaning 'strong as a wolf'.

Wolfgang
Teutonic, meaning 'the path of wolves'. Composer Mozart's full name was Wolfgang Amadeus Mozart.

Wolfrom
Teutonic, meaning 'raven wolf'.

Wolter
Dutch, a form of Walter meaning 'ruler of the army'.

Woodburn
Old English, meaning 'a stream in the woods'.

Woodrow
English, meaning 'from the row of houses by the wood'.

Food-inspired names

Ale
Basil
Berry
Cane
Chuck
Graham
Herb
Kale
Reuben
Rye
Shad
Tamir

Woodward
English, meaning 'guardian of the forest'.

Woody
American, meaning 'path in the woods'.

Worcester
Old English, meaning 'from a Roman site'.

Worth
American, meaning 'worth much' or 'wealthy place' or 'wealth and riches'.

Wren
Old English, meaning 'tiny bird'.

Wright
Old English, meaning 'to be a craftsman' or 'from a carpenter'.

Wyatt
Teutonic, meaning 'from wood' or 'from the wide water'.

Wynn
(alt. Wyn)
Welsh, meaning 'very blessed' or 'the fair blessed one'.

Popular English names for boys and girls

Ada	Julian
Darren	Lana
Dudley	Lauren
Faith	Posy
Garrett	Rodney

Boys' names

Xadrian
American, a combination of X and Adrian, meaning 'from Hadria'.

Xander
Greek, meaning 'defender of the people'.

Xanthus
Greek, meaning 'golden-haired'.

Xavier
Latin, meaning 'to the new house'.

Xenon
Greek, meaning 'the guest'.

Xerxes
Persian, meaning 'ruler of the people' or 'respected king'. Name of several important Persian kings.

Xylander
Greek, meaning 'man of the forest'.

Bird names

Drake
Efron
Gannet
Hawke
Jay
Lorian
Manu
Robin
Sparrow
Talon

Names of Presidents

Abraham (Lincoln)
Andrew (Jackson, Johnson)
Barack (Obama)
Franklin (Pierce, Roosevelt)
George (Washington, H. Bush, W. Bush)
James (Madison, Monroe, Knox Polk, Buchanan, Garfield, Carter)
John (Adams, Quincy Adams, Tyler, Kennedy)
Richard (Nixon)
Ronald (Reagan)
William (Henry Harrison, McKinley, Howard Taft, Clinton)

Y

Yaal
Hebrew, meaning 'ascending' or 'one to ascend'.

Yadid
Hebrew, meaning 'the beloved one'.

Yadon
Hebrew, meaning 'against judgment'.

Yahir
Spanish, meaning 'handsome one'.

Yair
Hebrew, meaning 'the enlightening one' or 'illuminating'.

Yakiya
Hebrew, meaning 'pure' or 'bright'.

Yanis
(alt. Yannis)
Greek, a form of John meaning 'gift of God'.

Yarden
Hebrew, meaning 'to flow downward'.

Ye
Chinese, meaning 'bright one' or 'light'.

Yehuda
Hebrew, meaning 'to praise and exalt'.

Yered
Hebrew, a form of Jared, meaning 'descending'.

Yerik
Russian, meaning 'God-appointed one'.

Y

Yervant
Armenian, meaning 'king of people'.

Yitzak
(alt. Yitzaak)
Hebrew, meaning 'laughter' or 'one who laughs'.

Ynyr
Welsh, meaning 'to honor'.

Yobachi
African, meaning 'one who prays to God' or 'prayed to God'.

Yogi
Japanese, meaning 'one who practices yoga' or 'from yoga'.

Yona
Native American, meaning 'bear'; Hebrew, meaning 'dove'.

York
Celtic, meaning 'yew tree' or 'from the farm of the yew tree'. Also a UK city.

Yosef
Hebrew, meaning 'added by God' or 'God shall add'.

Yuri
Aboriginal, meaning 'to hear'; Japanese, meaning 'one to listen'; Russian, a form of George meaning 'farmer'.

Yves
French, meaning 'miniature archer' or 'small archer'.

Z Boys' names

Zachariah
(alt. Zac, Zach, Zachary)
Hebrew, meaning 'remembered by the Lord' or 'God has remembered'.

Zad
Persian, meaning 'my son'.

Zadok
Hebrew, meaning 'righteous one'. *Zadok the Priest* is a well-known coronation anthem and has been sung at every crowning of a king or queen in the UK since 1727.

Zador
Hungarian, meaning 'violent demeanor'.

Zafar
Arabic, meaning 'triumphant'.

Zaid
African, meaning 'increase the growth' or 'growth'.

Zaide
Yiddish, meaning 'the elder ones'.

Zain
(alt. Zane)
Arabic, meaning 'the handsome son'.

Zaire
African, meaning 'river from Zaire'.

Zander
Greek, meaning 'defender of my people'.

Z

Zarek
Persian, meaning 'God protect our king'.

Zuma
Arabic, meaning 'peace'.

Names from nature

Ash
Berry
Condor
Flint
Glenn
Linden
River
Reed
Rock
Tiger

part three

Girls' Names

A Girls' names

A'mari
Variation of the Swahili or Muslim name Amira, meaning 'princess'.

Aanya
Sanskrit, meaning 'the inexhaustible'.

Aaryanna
Variation of Ariadne, meaning 'the very holy one'.

Abigail
(alt. Abagail, Abbigail, Abbey, Abbie, Abby, Abigale, Abigayle)
Hebrew, meaning 'my father's joy'.

Abilene
(alt. Abelena, Abilee)
Latin and Spanish, meaning 'hazelnut'.

Abra
Female variation of Abraham. Also Sanskrit, meaning 'clouds'.

Abril
Spanish for the month of April; Latin, meaning 'open'.

Acacia
Greek, meaning 'point' or 'thorn'. Also a species of flowering trees and shrubs.

Acadia
Greek, meaning 'paradise'. Originally, a French colony in Canada.

Ada
(alt. Adair, Adia)
Hebrew, meaning 'adornment'.

Adalee
German, meaning 'noble'.

Adalia
Hebrew, meaning 'God is my refuge'.

Addie
(alt. Addy, Adi)
Shortened form of Addison, Adelaide, Adele and Adeline.

Addison
(alt. Addisyn, Addyson)
English, meaning 'son of Adam'.

Adelaide
(alt. Adelaida)
Old German, meaning 'noble kind'. Popular after the rule of William IV and Queen Adelaide of England in the 19th century.

Adele
(alt. Adela, Adelia, Adell, Adella, Adelle)
German, meaning 'noble' or 'nobility'.

Adeline
(alt. Adalyn, Adalynn, Adelina, Adelyn)
Variant of Adelaide, meaning 'noble'.

Aden
(alt. Addien)
Hebrew, meaning 'decoration'.

Aderyn
Welsh, meaning 'bird'.

Adesina
Nigerian, meaning 'she paves the way'. Usually given to a first-born daughter.

Movie inspirations

Anita (*West Side Story*)
Bonnie (*Bonnie & Clyde*)
Dorothy (*The Wizard of Oz*)
Holly (*Breakfast at Tiffany's*)
Judy (*Private Benjamin*)
Leia (*Star Wars*)
Mary (*Mary Poppins*)
Oda Mae (*Ghost*)
Ripley (*Alien*)
Sandy (*Grease*)

Adina
(alt. Adena)
Hebrew, meaning 'high hopes' or 'precious'.

Adira
Hebrew, meaning 'noble' or 'powerful'. Also the north Italian city.

Adrian
Italian, from the northern city of Adria.

Adrienne
(alt. Adriane, Adriana, Adrianna, Adrianne)
Greek, meaning 'rich', or Latin meaning 'dark'.

Aegle
Greek, meaning 'brightness' or 'splendor'.

Aerin
Variant of Erin, meaning 'peace-making'.

Aerith
American, with no definitive meaning.

Aero
(alt. Aeron)
Greak, meaning 'water'.

Aerolynn
Combination of the Greek Aero, meaning 'water', and the English Lynn, meaning 'waterfall'.

Africa
Celtic, meaning 'pleasant', as well as the name of the continent.

Afsaneh
Iranian, meaning 'a fairy tale'.

Afsha
Persian, meaning 'one who sprinkles light'.

Afton
Originally a place name in Scotland.

Agatha
From Saint Agatha, the patron saint of bells, meaning 'good'.

Aglaia
Greek, meaning 'brilliance'. One of the three Greek graces.

Agnes
Greek, meaning 'virginal' or 'pure'.

Agrippina
Latin, meaning 'born feet first'.

Aida
Arabic, meaning 'reward' or 'present'.

Aidanne
(alt. Aidan, Aidenn)
Gaelic, meaning 'fire'.

Ailbhe
Irish, meaning 'noble' or 'bright'.

Aileen
(alt. Aelinn, Aleen, Aline, Alline, Eileen)
Gaelic variant of Helen, meaning 'light'.

Ailith
(alt. Ailish)
Old English, meaning 'seasoned warrior'.

Ailsa
Scottish, meaning 'pledge from God'. Also the name of a Scottish island.

Aimee
(alt. Aimie, Amie)
French form of Amy, meaning 'beloved'.

Aina
Scandinavian, meaning 'forever'.

Aine
(alt. Aino)
Celtic, meaning 'happiness'.

Ainsley
Scottish/Gaelic, meaning 'one's own meadow'.

Aisha
(alt. Aeysha)
Arabic, meaning 'woman';
Swahili, meaning 'life'.

Aishwarya
Arabic, meaning 'woman'.

Aislinn
(alt. Aislin, Aisling, Aislyn, Alene, Allene)
Irish Gaelic, meaning 'dream'.

Aiyanna
(alt. Aiyana)
Native American, meaning 'forever flowering'.

Aja
Hindi, meaning 'goat'.

Akela
(alt. Akilah)
Hawaiian, meaning 'noble'.

Akilina
Greek or Russian, meaning 'eagle'.

Akiva
Hebrew, meaning 'protect and shelter'.

Alaina

*(alt. Alana, Alane, Alani, Alanna,
Allannah, Alayna, Aleena)*
Feminine of Alan, originating
from the Greek for 'rock' or
'comely'.

Alanis

(alt. Alarice)
Greek, meaning 'rock' or
'comely'.

Alba

Latin for 'white'.

Alberta

(alt. Albertha, Albertine)
Feminine of Albert, from the
Old German for 'noble, bright,
famous'.

Albina

Latin, meaning 'white' or 'fair'.

Alda

German, meaning 'old' or
'prosperous'.

Aldis

English, meaning 'battle-
seasoned'.

Aleta

(alt. Aletha)
Greek, meaning 'footloose'.

Alethea

(alt. Aletheia)
Greek, meaning 'truth'.

Alex

*(alt. Alexa, Alexi, Alexia, Alexina,
Ali, Allie, Ally)*
Shortened version of
Alexandra, meaning 'man's
defender'.

Alexandra

*(alt. Alejandra, Alejandrina,
Alejhandra, Aleksandra,
Alessandra, Alexandrea,
Alexandria, Aliandra)*
Feminine of Alexander,
from the Greek interpretation
of 'man's defender'.

Alexis

(alt. Alexus, Alexys)
Greek, meaning 'helper'.

Aleydis

Variant of Alice, meaning
'nobility'.

Alfreda

Old English, meaning 'elf
power'.

Alibeth

Variant of Elizabeth, meaning
'pledged to God'.

Alice

(alt. Alize, Alyce, Alys, Alyse)
English, meaning 'noble' or
'nobility'.

Alicia
(alt. Ahlicia, Alecia, Alesia, Alessia, Alizia, Alycia, Alysia)
Variant of Alice, meaning 'nobility'.

Alida
(alt. Aleida)
Latin, meaning 'small-winged one'.

Alienor
(alt. Aliana)
Variant of Eleanor. Greek, meaning 'light'.

Aliki
(alt. Alika)
Variant of Alice, meaning 'nobility'.

Alima
Arabic, meaning 'cultured'.

Alina
(alt. Alena, Aleana)
Slavic form of Helen, meaning 'light'.

Alisha
(alt. Alesha, Alysha)
Variant of Alice, meaning 'nobility'.

Alison
(alt. Allison, Allisyn, Allyson, Alyson)
Variant of Alice, meaning 'nobility'.

Alivia
Variant of Olivia, meaning 'olive tree'.

Aliya
(alt. Aaliyah, Aleah, Alia, Aliah, Aliyah)
Arabic, meaning 'exalted' or 'sublime'.

Alla
Variant of Ella or Alexandra. Also a possible reference to Allah.

Allegra
Italian, meaning 'joyous'.

Allura
French, from the word for entice, meaning 'the power of attraction'.

Allyn
Feminine of Alan, meaning 'peaceful'.

Alma
Latin for 'giving nurture'; Italian for 'soul'; and Arabic for 'learned'.

Almeda
(alt. Almeta)
Latin, meaning 'ambitious'.

Almera
(alt. Almira)
Feminine of Elmer, from the Arabic for 'aristocratic'; Old English meaning 'noble'.

Alohi
Variant of the Hawaiian greeting Aloha, meaning 'love and affection'.

Alona
Hebrew, meaning 'oak tree'.

Alora
Variant of Alona, meaning 'oak tree'.

Alpha
The first letter of the Greek alphabet, usually given to a firstborn daughter.

Alta
Latin, meaning 'elevated'.

Altagracia
Spanish, meaning 'grace'.

Althea
(alt. Altea, Altha)
Greek, meaning 'healing power'.

Alva
Spanish, meaning 'blonde' or 'fair-skinned'.

Alvena
(alt. Alvina)
English, meaning 'noble friend'.

Alvia
(alt. Alyvia)
Variant of Olivia or Elvira.

Alyssa
(alt. Alisa, Alissa, Allyssa, Alysa)
Greek, meaning 'rational'.

Amadea
Feminine of Amadeus, meaning 'God's' love.

Amalia
Variant of Emilia, Latin, meaning 'rival, eager'.

Amana
Hebrew, meaning 'loyal and true'.

Amanda
(alt. Amandine)
Latin, meaning 'much loved'.

Amara
(alt. Amani)
Greek, meaning 'lovely forever'.

Amarantha
Contraction of Amanda and Samantha, meaning 'much loved listener'.

Amaris
(alt. Amari, Amasa, Amata, Amaya)
Hebrew, meaning 'pledged by God'.

Amaryllis
(alt. Ameris)
Greek, meaning 'fresh'. Also a flower by the same name.

Amber
French, from the semi-precious stone of the same name.

Amberly
Contraction of Amber and Leigh, meaning 'stone' and 'meadow'.

Amberlynn
Contraction of Amber and Lynn, meaning 'stone' and 'waterfall'.

Amelia
(alt. Aemilia)
Greek, meaning 'industrious'.

Amelie
(alt. Amalie)
French version of Amelia, meaning 'industrious'.

America
From the country of the same name.

Amethyst
Greek, from the precious, mulberry colored stone of the same name.

Amina
Arabic, meaning 'honest and trustworthy'.

Amira
(alt. Amiya, Amiyah)
Arabic, meaning 'a high-born girl'.

Amity
Latin, meaning 'friendship and harmony'.

Amory
Variant of the Spanish name Amor, meaning 'love'.

Amy
(alt. Aimee, Amee, Ami, Amie, Ammie, Amya)
Latin, meaning 'beloved'.

Ana-Lisa
Contraction of Anna and Lisa, meaning 'grace' or 'consecrated to God'.

Anafa
Hebrew, meaning 'heron'.

Ananda
Hindi, meaning 'bliss'.

Anastasia
(alt. Athanasia)
Greek, meaning 'resurrection'.

Anatolia

From the eastern Greek town of the same name.

Andrea

(alt. Andreia, Andria)
Feminine of Andrew, from the Greek term for 'a man's woman'.

Andrine

Variant of Andrea, meaning 'a man's woman'.

Andromeda

From the heroine of a Greek legend.

Anemone

Greek, meaning 'breath'.

Angela

(alt. Angel, Angeles, Angelia Angelle, Angie)
Greek, meaning 'messenger from God' or 'angel'.

Angelica

(alt. Angelina, Angeline, Angelique, Angelise, Angelita, Anjelica, Anjelina)
Latin, meaning 'angelic'.

Anise

(alt. Anisa, Anissa)
French, from the licorice flavored plant of the same name.

Aniston

English, meaning 'town of Agnes'. Last name of actress Jennifer Aniston.

Anita

(alt. Anitra)
Variant of Ann, meaning 'grace'.

Ann

(alt. Anne)
Derived from Hannah, meaning 'grace'.

Anna

(alt. Ana)
Derived from Hannah, meaning 'grace'.

Annabel

(alt. Anabel, Anabelle, Annabell, Annabella, Annabelle, Amabel)
Contraction of Anna and Belle, meaning 'grace' and 'beauty'.

Annalise

(alt. Annalee, Annalisa, Anneli, Annelie, Annelise)
Contraction of Anna and Lise, meaning 'grace' and 'pledged to God'.

Annemarie

(alt. Annamae, Annamarie, Annelle, Annmarie)
Contraction of Anna and Mary, meaning 'grace' and 'star of the sea'.

Annette
(alt. Annetta)
Hebrew, derived from Hannah, meaning 'grace'.

Annis
Greek, meaning 'finished or completed'.

Annora
Latin, meaning 'honor'.

Anoushka
(alt. Anousha)
Russian variation of Ann, meaning 'grace'.

Ansley
English, meaning 'the awesome one's meadow'.

Anthea
(alt. Anthi)
Greek, meaning 'flower-like'.

Antigone
In Greek mythology, Antigone was the daughter of Oedipus.

Antoinette
(alt. Anonetta, Antonette, Antonietta)
Female form of Anthony, meaning 'invaluable grace'.

Antonia
(alt. Antonella, Antonina)
Latin, meaning 'invaluable'.

Anwen
Welsh, meaning 'very fair'.

Anya
(alt. Aniya, Aniyah, Aniylah, Anja)
Russian, meaning 'grace'.

Aoife
Gaelic, meaning 'beautiful joy'.

Apollonia
Feminine of Apollo, the Greek god of the sun.

Apple
From the name of the fruit.

April
(alt. Avril)
Latin, meaning 'opening up'. Also the fourth month.

Aquilina
(alt. Aqua, Aquila)
Spanish, meaning 'like an eagle'.

Ara
Arabic, meaning 'brings rain'.

Arabella
(alt. Arabelle)
Latin, meaning 'answered prayer'.

Araceli
(alt. Aracely)
Spanish, meaning 'altar of Heaven'.

Araminta
Contraction of Arabella and Amita, meaning 'altar of Heaven' and 'friendship'.

Arcadia
Greek, meaning 'paradise'.

Ardelle
(alt. Ardell, Ardella)
Latin, meaning 'burning with enthusiasm'.

Arden
(alt. Ardis, Ardith)
Latin, meaning 'burning with enthusiasm'.

Arella
(alt. Areli, Arely)
Hebrew, meaning 'angel'.

Aretha
Greek, meaning 'woman of virtue'.

Aria
(alt. Ariah)
Italian, meaning 'melody'.

Ariadne
Both Greek and Latin, meaning 'the very holy one'. In Greek mythology, Ariadne was the daughter of King Minos.

Ariana
(alt. Ariane, Arianna, Arienne)
Welsh, meaning 'silver'.

Ariel
(alt. Ariela, Ariella, Arielle)
Hebrew, meaning 'lioness of God'.

Arlene
(alt. Arleen, Arlie, Arline, Arly)
Gaelic, meaning 'pledge'.

Armida
Latin, meaning 'little armed one'.

Artemisia
(alt. Artemis, Arti, Artie)
Greek/Spanish, meaning 'perfect'.

Artie
(alt. Arti)
Shortened form of Artemisia, meaning 'perfect'.

Ashanti
Geographical area in Africa. Also the name of a popular R&B singer.

Ashby
English, meaning 'ash tree farm'.

Ashley
(alt. Ashlee, Ashleigh, Ashli, Ashlie, Ashly)
English, meaning 'ash tree meadow'.

Ashlynn
(alt. Ashlyn)
Irish Gaelic, meaning 'dream'.

Ashton
(alt. Ashtyn)
Old English, meaning 'ash tree town'.

Asia
Name of the continent.

Asma
(alt. Asmara)
Arabic, meaning 'high-standing'.

Aspen
(alt. Aspynn)
Name of the tree. Also the city famous for its ski resort.

Assumpta
(alt. Assunta)
Italian, meaning 'raised up'.

Asta
(alt. Asteria, Astor, Astoria)
Greek or Latin, meaning 'star-like'.

Astrid
Old Norse, meaning 'beautiful like a God'.

Atara
Hebrew, meaning 'diadem'.

Athena
(alt. Athenais)
The Greek goddess of wisdom.

Aubrey
(alt. Aubree, Aubriana, Aubrie)
French, meaning 'elf ruler'.

Audrey
(alt. Audra, Audrie, Audrina, Audry)
English, meaning 'noble strength'.

Augusta
(alt. August, Augustine)
Latin, meaning 'worthy of respect'.

Aura
(alt. Aurea)
Greek or Latin, meaning either 'soft breeze' or 'gold'.

Aurelia
(alt. Aurelie)
Latin, meaning gold.

Aurora
(alt. Aurore)
In Roman mythology, Aurora was the goddess of sunrise.

Austine
(alt. Austen, Austin)
Latin, meaning 'worthy of respect'.

Autumn
Name of the season.

Ava
(alt. Avia, Avie)
Latin, meaning 'like a bird'.

Avalon
(alt. Avalyn, Aveline)
Celtic, meaning 'island of apples'.

Axelle
Greek, meaning 'father of peace'.

Aya
(alt. Ayah)
Hebrew, meaning 'bird'.

Ayanna
(alt. Ayana)
American, meaning 'grace'.

Ayesha
(alt. Aisha, Aysha)
Persian, meaning 'small one'.

Azalea
Latin, meaning 'dry earth'. Also the name of a flowering shrub.

Azalia
Hebrew, meaning 'aided by God'.

Aziza
Hebrew, meaning 'mighty', or Arabic meaning 'precious'.

Azure
(alt. Azaria)
French, meaning 'sky-blue'.

Popular French names for boys and girls

Adele
Alain
Alphonse
Belle
Fleur
Jacques
Marc
Mathieu
Paulette
Sabine

A

B Girls' names

Babette
(alt. Babe)
French version of Barbara,
Greek meaning 'foreign'.

Bailey
(alt. Baeli, Bailee)
English, meaning 'law
enforcer'.

Bambi
(alt. Bambina)
Shortened version of the
Italian Bambina, meaning
'child'.

Barbara
(alt. Barb, Barbie, Barbra)
Greek, meaning 'foreign'.

Basma
Arabic, meaning 'smile'.

Bathsheba
Hebrew, meaning 'daughter of
the oath'. Bathsheba was a key
biblical figure, and mother of
King Solomon.

Bay
(alt. Baya)
Plant or geographical name.

Beata
Latin, meaning 'blessed'.

Beatrice
*(alt. Bea, Beatrix, Beatriz, Bee,
Bellatrix)*
Latin, meaning 'bringer of
gladness'.

Becky
(alt. Beccie, Beccy, Beckie)
Shortened form of Rebecca,
meaning 'joined'.

Literary names

Alice (*Alice in Wonderland*, Lewis Carroll)
Beth (*Little Women*, Louisa M. Alcott)
Cora (*Last of the Mohicans*, James Fenimore Cooper)
Eliza (*Pygmalion*, George Bernard Shaw)
Gwendolen (*The Importance of Being Earnest*, Oscar Wilde)
Hermione (Harry Potter series, J. K. Rowling)
Isabella (Twilight series, Stephenie Meyer)
Matilda (*Matilda*, Roald Dahl)
Miranda (*The Tempest*, William Shakespeare)
Wendy (*Peter Pan*, J. M. Barrie)

Belinda
(alt. Belen, Belina)
Contraction of Belle and Linda, meaning 'beautiful'.

Bella
Latin, meaning 'beautiful'.

Belle
(alt. Bell)
French, meaning 'beautiful'. Popularized by the Disney princess in *Beauty and the Beast*.

Belva
Latin, meaning 'beautiful view'.

Bénédicta
Latin, the feminine of Benedict, meaning 'blessed'.

Benita
(alt. Bernita)
Spanish, meaning 'blessed'.

Bennie
Shortened form of Bénédicta and Benita.

Berit
(alt. Beret)
Scandinavian, meaning 'splendid' or 'gorgeous'.

Bernadette
French, meaning 'courageous'.

Bernadine
French, meaning 'courageous'.

B

Bernice
(alt. Berenice, Berniece, Burnice)
Greek, meaning 'she who brings victory'.

Bertha
(alt. Berta, Berthe, Bertie)
German, meaning 'bright'.

Beryl
Greek, meaning 'pale, green gemstone'.

Bess
(alt. Bessie)
Shortened form of Elizabeth, meaning 'consecrated to God'.

Beth
Hebrew, meaning 'house'. Also shortened form of Elizabeth, meaning 'consecrated to God'.

Bethany
(alt. Bethan)
Hebrew, referring to a geographical location.

Bethel
Hebrew, meaning 'house of God'.

Bettina
Spanish version of Elizabeth, meaning 'consecrated to God'.

Betty
(alt. Betsy, Bette, Bettie, Bettye)
Shortened version of Elizabeth, meaning 'consecrated to God'.

Beulah
Hebrew, meaning 'married'.

Beverly
(alt. Beverlee, Beverley)
English, meaning 'beaver stream'.

Beyoncé
American, made popular by the singer.

Bianca
(alt. Blanca)
Italian, meaning 'white'.

Bijou
French, meaning 'precious ring'.

Billie
(alt. Bill, Billy, Billye)
Shortened version of Wilhelmina, meaning 'determined'.

Bina
Hebrew, meaning 'knowledge'.

Birgit
(alt. Birgitta)
Norwegian, meaning 'splendid'.

217

Blaer
Icelandic, meaning 'light breeze'.

Blair
Scottish Gaelic, meaning 'flat, plain area'.

Blake
(alt. Blakely, Blakelyn)
English, meaning either 'pale-skinned' or 'dark'.

Blanche
(alt. Blanch)
French, meaning 'white or pale'.

Bliss
English, meaning 'intense happiness'.

Blithe
English, meaning 'joyous'.

Blodwen
Welsh, meaning 'white flower'.

Blossom
English, meaning 'flowerlike'.

Blythe
(alt. Bly)
English, meaning 'happy and carefree'.

Bobbi
(alt. Bobbie, Bobby)
Shortened version of Roberta, meaning 'bright fame'.

Bonita
Spanish, meaning 'pretty'.

Bonnie
(alt. Bonny)
Scottish, meaning 'fair of face'.

Brandy
(alt. Brandee, Brandi, Brandie)
Dutch, meaning 'burnt wine'. Name of the liquor.

Brea
(alt. Bree, Bria)
Shortened form of Brianna, meaning 'strong'.

Brenda
English, meaning 'burning or stinking hair'.

Biblical names

Elizabeth
Eve
Hannah
Leah
Mary
Miriam
Rachel
Rebecca
Ruth
Sarah

Brianna
(alt. *Breana, Breann, Breanna, Breanne, Brenna, Brenyn, Briana, Brianne, Bryanna*)
Irish Gaelic, meaning 'strong'.

Bridget
(alt. *Bridgett, Bridgette, Brigette, Brigid, Brigitta, Brigitte*)
Irish Gaelic, meaning 'strength and power'.

Brier
French, meaning 'heather'.

Brit
(alt. *Britt, Britta*)
Celtic, meaning 'spotted' or 'freckled'.

Britannia
Latin, meaning 'Britain'.

Brittany
(alt. *Britany, Britney, Britni, Brittani, Brittanie, Brittney, Brittni, Brittny*)
Latin, meaning 'from England'. Also the name of a French city.

Bronwyn
(alt. *Bronwen*)
Welsh, meaning 'fair breast'.

Brooke
(alt. *Brook*)
English, meaning 'small stream'.

Brooklyn
(alt. *Brooklynn*)
Name of a New York borough.

Brunhilda
German, meaning 'armor-wearing fighting maid'.

Bryn
(alt. *Brynn*)
Welsh, meaning 'mount'.

Bryony
(alt. *Briony*)
Name of a European vine.

Popular Indian names for boys and girls

Ajay
Bharat
Deepal
Haresh
Jaya
Manisha
Paresh
Rabiya
Ravi
Sunita

B

C Girls' names

Cadence
Latin, meaning 'with rhythm'.

Cai
Vietnamese, meaning 'feminine'.

Caitlin
(alt. Cadyn, Caitlann, Caitlyn, Caitlynn)
Greek, meaning 'pure'.

Calandra
Greek, meaning 'lark'.

Calantha
(alt. Calanthe)
Greek, meaning 'lovely flower'.

Caledonia
Latin, meaning 'from Scotland'.

Calla
Greek, meaning 'beautiful'.

Callie
(alt. Caleigh, Cali, Calleigh, Cally)
Greek, meaning 'beauty'.

Calliope
Greek, meaning 'beautiful voice'. From the muse of epic poetry in Greek mythology.

Callista
(alt. Callisto)
Greek, meaning 'most beautiful'.

Camas
Native American, from the root and bulb of the same name.

Cambria
Welsh, from the alternate name for Wales.

Camden
(alt. Camdyn)
English, meaning 'winding valley'.

Cameo
Italian, meaning 'skin'.

Cameron
(alt. Camryn)
Scottish Gaelic, meaning 'bent nose'.

Camilla
(alt. Camelia, Camellia, Camila, Camille, Camillia)
Latin, meaning 'spiritual serving girl'.

Candace
(alt. Candice, Candis)
Latin, meaning 'brilliant white'.

Candida
Latin, meaning 'white'.

Candra
Latin, meaning 'glowing'.

Candy
(alt. Candi)
Shortened form of Candace, meaning 'brilliant white'.

Caoimhe
Celtic, meaning 'gentleness'. Has many different pronounciations, including

'Kyva' and 'Keeva', depending on where in Ireland you hear it.

Caprice
Italian, meaning 'ruled by whim'.

Cara
Latin, meaning 'darling'.

Caren
(alt. Carin, Caron, Caryn)
Greek, meaning 'pure'.

Carey
(alt. Cari, Carie, Carri, Carrie, Cary)
Welsh, meaning 'near the castle'.

Carina
(alt. Corina)
Italian, meaning 'dearest little one'.

Carissa
(alt. Carisa)
Greek, meaning 'grace'.

Carla
(alt. Charla)
Feminine of the Old Norse Carl, meaning 'free man'.

Carlin
(alt. Carleen, Carlene)
Gaelic, meaning 'little champion'.

C

Popular American names for girls

Addison	Kendra
Aubree	Lacey
Avery	Madison
Harper	Misty
Kayla	Zoey

Carlotta
(alt. Carlota)
Italian, meaning 'free man'.

Carly
(alt. Carlee, Carley, Carli, Carlie)
Feminine of the German
Charles, meaning 'man'.

Carmel
*(alt. Carmela, Carmelita,
Carmella)*
Hebrew, meaning 'garden'.

Carmen
(alt. Carma, Carmina)
Latin, meaning 'song'. Name of
a popular opera and ballet by
composer Georges Bizet.

Carol
*(alt. Carole, Carrol, Carroll,
Caryl)*
Shortened form of Caroline,
meaning 'man'.

Caroline
*(alt. Carolann, Carolina,
Carolyn, Carolynn)*
German, meaning 'man'.

Carrington
English, meaning 'Charles's
town'.

Carys
(alt. Cerys)
Welsh, meaning 'love'.

Casey
(alt. Casy, Casie)
Irish Gaelic, meaning
'watchful'.

Cassandra
(alt. Casandra, Cassandre)
Greek, meaning 'one who
prophesies doom'.

Cassia
(alt. Casia, Casie, Cassie)
Greek, meaning 'cinnamon'.

C

Saints' names

Ada
Agatha
Catherine
Felicity
Helena
Joan
Lydia
Margaret
Mary
Teresa

Cassidy
Irish, meaning 'clever'.

Catalina
(alt. Catarina, Caterina)
Spanish version of Catherine, meaning 'pure'.

Catherine
(alt. Catharine, Cathrine, Cathryn)
Greek, meaning 'pure'.
Catherine the Great was the longest serving female ruler of Russia from 1762 until 1796.

Cathleen
Irish version of Catherine, meaning 'pure'.

Cathy
(alt. Cathey, Cathi, Cathie)
Shortened form of Catherine, meaning 'pure'.

Caty
(alt. Caddie, Caitee, Caitie, Cate, Catie)
Shortened form of Catherine, meaning 'pure'.

Cayley
(alt. Cayla, Caylee, Caylen)
American, meaning 'pure'.

Cecilia
(alt. Cecelia, Cecile, Cecilie, Cecily, Cicely, Cicily)
Latin, meaning 'blind one'.

Celena
Greek, meaning 'goddess of the moon'.

Celeste
(alt. Celestina, Celestine)
Latin, meaning 'heavenly'.

Celine
(alt. Celia, Celina)
French version of Celeste, meaning 'heavenly'.

Cerise
French, meaning 'cherry'.

Chanah
Hebrew, meaning 'grace'.

C

Chance
Middle English, meaning 'good fortune'.

Chandler
(alt. Chandell)
English, meaning 'candle maker'.

Chandra
(alt. Chanda, Chandry)
Sanskrit, meaning 'like the moon'.

Chanel
(alt. Chanelle)
French, from the designer of the same name.

Chantal
(alt. Chantel, Chantelle, Chantilly)
French, meaning 'stony spot'.

Chardonnay
French, from the wine variety of the same name.

Charis
(alt. Charice, Charissa, Charisse)
Greek, meaning 'grace'.

Charity
Latin, meaning 'brotherly love'.

Charlene
(alt. Charleen, Charline)
German, meaning 'man'.

Charlie
(alt. Charlee, Charley, Charlize, Charly)
Shortened form of Charlotte, meaning 'little and feminine'.

Charlotte
(alt. Charnette, Charolette)
French, meaning 'little and feminine'. Briefly became popular after the publication of Charlotte's Web by E. B. White.

Charmaine
Latin, meaning 'clan'.

Chastity
Latin, meaning 'purity'.

Chava
(alt. Chaya)
Hebrew, meaning 'beloved'.

Chelsea
(alt. Chelsee, Chelsey, Chelsi, Chelsie)
English, meaning 'port or landing place'.

Cher
French, meaning 'beloved'.

Cherie
(alt. Cheri, Cherise)
French, meaning 'dear'.

C

Cherish
(alt. Cherith)
English, meaning 'to treasure'.

Chermona
Hebrew, meaning 'sacred mountain'.

Cherry
(alt. Cherri)
French, meaning 'cherry fruit'.

Cheryl
(alt. Cheryle)
English, meaning 'little and womanly'.

Chesney
English, meaning 'place to camp'.

Cheyenne
(alt. Cheyanne)
Native American, from the tribe of the same name.

Chiara
(alt. Ceara, Chiarina, Ciara)
Italian, meaning 'light'.

China
From the country of the same name.

Chiquita
Spanish, meaning 'little one'.

Chloe
(alt. Cloe)
Greek, meaning 'pale green shoot'.

Chloris
(alt. Cloris)
Greek, meaning 'pale'. Made famous by actress and comedian Cloris Leachman.

TV personality names

Brooke (Burke Charvet)
Cat (Deeley)
Connie (Chung)
Ellen (DeGeneres)
Giada (De Laurentiis)
Giuliana (Rancic)
Oprah (Winfrey)
Padma (Lakshmi)
Samantha (Harris)
Tyra (Banks)

C

Chris
*(alt. Chrissy, Christa, Christie,
Christy, Crissy, Cristy)*
Shortened form of Christina,
meaning 'anointed Christian'.

Christabel
(alt. Christobel)
Latin and French, meaning 'fair
Christian'.

Christina
(alt. Christiana, Cristina)
Greek, meaning 'anointed
Christian'.

Christine
*(alt. Christeen, Christen,
Christene, Christian, Christiane,
Christin)*
Greek, meaning 'anointed
Christian'.

Chuma
Aramaic, meaning 'warmth'.

Cierra
(alt. Ciera)
Irish, meaning 'black'.

Cinderella
French, meaning 'little ash-
girl'. Subject of a well-known
children's fairy tale.

Cindy
(alt. Cinda, Cindi, Cyndi)
Shortened form of Cynthia,
meaning 'goddess from the
mountain'.

Cinnamon
Greek, from the spice of the
same name.

Citlali
(alt. Citlalli)
Aztec, meaning 'star'.

Citrine
Latin, from the gemstone of the
same name.

Claire
(alt. Clara, Clare, Claira)
Latin, meaning 'bright'.

Clarabelle
(alt. Claribel)
Contraction of Clare and
Isobel, meaning 'bright' and
'consecrated to God'.

Clarissa
(alt. Clarice, Clarisse)
Variation of Claire, meaning
'bright'.

Clarity
Latin, meaning 'lucid'.

Claudette
(alt. Claudetta)
Latin, meaning 'lame'.

Claudia
(alt. Claudie, Claudine)
Latin, meaning 'lame'.

C

227

Clematis
Greek, meaning 'vine'.

Clementine
(alt. Clemency, Clementina, Clemmie)
Latin, meaning 'mild and merciful'. Also the small orange fruit.

Cleopatra
Greek, meaning 'her father's renown'.

Clio
(alt. Cleo, Cliona)
Greek, from the muse of the same name.

Clodagh
Irish, meaning 'river'.

Clotilda
(alt. Clothilda, Clothilde, Clotilde)
German, meaning 'renowned battle'.

Clover
English, from the flower of the same name.

Coco
Spanish, meaning 'help'.

Cody
English, meaning 'pillow'.

Colleen
(alt. Coleen)
Irish Gaelic, meaning 'girl'.

Collette
(alt. Colette)
Greek/French, meaning 'people of victory'.

Connie
Latin, meaning 'steadfast'.

Constance
(alt. Constanza)
Latin, meaning 'steadfast'.

Consuelo
(alt. Consuela)
Spanish, meaning 'comfort'.

Cora
Greek, meaning 'maiden'.

Coral
(alt. Coralie, Coraline, Corelia, Corene)
Latin, from the marine life of the same name.

Corazon
Spanish, meaning 'heart'.

Cordelia
(alt. Cordia, Cordie)
Latin, meaning 'heart'.

Corey
(alt. Cori, Corrie, Cory)
Irish Gaelic, meaning 'the hollow'.

Corin
(alt. Corine)
Latin, meaning 'spear'.

Corinne
(alt. Corinna, Corrine)
French version of Cora, meaning 'maiden'.

Corliss
English, meaning 'cheery'.

Cornelia
Latin, meaning 'like a horn'.

Cosette
French, meaning 'people of victory'. Name of a key character in Victor Hugo's Les Misérables.

Cosima
(alt. Cosmina)
Greek, meaning 'order'.

Courtney
(alt. Cortney)
English, meaning 'court-dweller'.

Creola
French, meaning 'American-born, English descent'.

Crescent
French, meaning 'increasing'.

Cressida
From the heroine in Greek mythology of the same name.

Crystal
(alt. Christal, Chrystal, Cristal)
Greek, meaning 'ice'.

Csilla
Hungarian, meaning 'defences'.

Cyd
Shortened form of Sidney, meaning 'wide island'.

Cynara
Greek, meaning 'thistly plant'.

Cynthia
Greek, meaning 'goddess from the mountain'.

Cyra
Persian, meaning 'sun'.

Cyrilla
Latin, meaning 'lordly'.

C

D Girls' names

Dacey
Irish Gaelic, meaning 'from the south'.

Dada
Nigerian, meaning 'curly haired'.

Daenerys
American, from the fictional character in the book *A Game of Thrones*.

Dagmar
German, meaning 'day's glory'.

Dagny
Nordic, meaning 'new day'.

Dahlia
Scandinavian, from the flower of the same name.

Dai
Japanese, meaning 'great'.

Daisy
(alt. Daisey, Dasia)
English, meaning 'eye of the day'.

Dakota
Native American, meaning 'allies'.

Dalia
(alt. Daliah, Dalila)
Hebrew, meaning 'delicate branch'.

Dallas
Scottish Gaelic, from the village of the same name. Also the city in Texas.

Damaris
Greek, meaning 'calf'.

Damita
Spanish, meaning 'little noblewoman'.

Dana
(alt. Dania, Danna, Dayna)
English, meaning 'from Denmark'.

Danae
Greek, from the mythological heroine of the same name.

Danica
(alt. Danika)
Latin, meaning 'from Denmark'.

Danielle
(alt. Danelle, Daniela, Daniella, Danila, Danyelle)
The feminine form of the Hebrew Daniel, meaning 'God is my judge'.

Danita
English, meaning 'God will judge'.

Daphne
(alt. Dafne, Daphna)
Greek, meaning 'laurel tree'. Daphne was a nymph associated with springs, fountains and wells in Greek mythology.

Dara
Hebrew/Persian, meaning 'wisdom'.

Darby
(alt. Darbi, Darbie)
Irish, meaning 'park with deer'.

Darcie
(alt. Darci, Darcy)
Irish Gaelic, meaning 'dark'.

Daria
Greek, meaning 'rich'.

Darla
English, meaning 'darling'.

Darlene
(alt. Darleen, Darline)
American, meaning 'darling'.

Daryl
(alt. Darryl)
English, originally used as a last name.

Davina
Hebrew, meaning 'loved one'.

Dawn
(alt. Dawna)
English, meaning 'the dawn'.

Daya
Hebrew, meaning 'bird of prey'.

Deanna
(alt. Dayana, Deana, Deanna, Deanne)
English, meaning 'valley'.

Deborah
(alt. Debbi, Debbie, Debbra, Debby, Debi, Debra, Debrah)
Hebrew, meaning 'bee'.

December
Latin, meaning 'tenth month'.

Dee
(alt. Dea)
Welsh, meaning 'swarthy'.

Deidre
(alt. Deidra, Deirdre)
Irish, meaning 'raging woman'.

Deja
(alt. Dejah)
French, meaning 'already'.

Delaney
(alt. Delany)
Irish Gaelic, meaning 'offspring of the challenger'.

Delia
Greek, meaning 'from Delos'.

Delilah
(alt. Delina)
Hebrew, meaning 'seductive'.

Della
(alt. Dell)
Shortened form of Adele, meaning 'nobility'.

Delores
(alt. Deloris)
Spanish, meaning 'sorrows'.

Delphine
(alt. Delpha, Delphia, Delphina, Delphinia)
Greek, meaning 'dolphin'.

Delta
Greek, meaning 'fourth child'.

Demetria
(alt. Demetrice, Dimitria)
Greek, from the mythological heroine of the same name.

Demi
French, meaning 'half'.

Dena
(alt. Deena)
English, meaning 'from the valley'.

Denise
(alt. Denice, Denisa, Denisse)
French, meaning 'follower of Dionysius'.

Desdemona
Greek, meaning 'wretchedness'. Desdemona is Othello's love interest in the Shakespearean play of the same name.

Desiree
(alt. Desirae)
French, meaning 'much desired'.

Desma
Greek, meaning 'blinding oath'.

Destiny
(alt. Destany, Destinee, Destiney, Destini)
French, meaning 'fate'.

Deva
Hindi, meaning 'God-like'.

Devin
(alt. Devinne)
Irish Gaelic, meaning 'poet'.

Devon
English, from the county of the same name.

Diamond
English, meaning 'brilliant'.

Diana
(alt. Dian, Diane, Dianna, Dianne)
Roman, meaning 'divine'.

Diandra
Greek, meaning 'two males'.

Dilys
Welsh, meaning 'reliable'.

Dimona
Hebrew, meaning 'south'.

Dinah
(alt. Dina)
Hebrew, meaning 'justified'.

Dionne
Greek, from the mythological heroine of the same name. The Dionne quintuplets were born in 1934 in Canada and remain perhaps the most famous of all quintuplet groups.

Divine
Italian, meaning 'heavenly'.

Dixie
French, meaning 'tenth'.

Dodie
Hebrew, meaning 'well-loved'.

Dolly
(alt. Dollie)
Shortened form of Dorothy, meaning 'gift of 'God'.

Dolores
(alt. Doloris)
Spanish, meaning 'sorrows'.

Uncommon three syllable names

Annabel	India
Cassandra	Juliet
Evelyn	Priscilla
Gloria	Tamara
Harriet	Vanessa

D

Dominique
(alt. Domenica, Dominica, Domonique)
Latin, meaning 'Lord'.

Donata
Latin, meaning 'given'.

Donna
(alt. Dona, Donnie)
Italian, meaning 'lady'.

Dora
Greek, meaning 'gift'.

Doran
Irish Gaelic, meaning 'fist' or 'stranger'.

Dorcas
Greek, meaning 'gazelle'.

Doreen
(alt. Dorene, Dorine)
Irish Gaelic, meaning 'brooding'.

Doris
(alt. Dorris)
Greek, from the place of the same name.

Dorothy
(alt. Dorathy, Doretha, Dorotha, Dorothea, Dorthy)
Greek, meaning 'gift of God'.

Dorrit
(alt. Dorit)
Greek, meaning 'gift of God'.
Little Dorrit is a novel by Charles Dickens.

Dory
(alt. Dori)
French, meaning 'gilded'.

Dottie
(alt. Dotty)
Shortened form of Dorothy, meaning 'gift of God'.

Dove
(alt. Dovie)
English, from the bird of the same name.

Drew
Greek, meaning 'masculine'.

Drusilla
(alt. Drucilla)
Latin, meaning 'of the Drusus clan'.

Dulcie
(alt. Dulce, Dulcia)
Latin, meaning 'sweet'.

Dusty
(alt. Dusti)
Old German, meaning 'brave warrior'.

E Girls' names

Earla
English, meaning 'leader'.

Eartha
English, meaning 'earth'.

Easter
Egyptian, from the festival of the same name.

Ebba
English, meaning 'fortress of riches'.

Ebony
(alt. Eboni)
Latin, meaning 'deep, black wood'.

Echo
Greek, meaning 'reflected sound'. From the mythological nymph of the same name.

Eda
(alt. Edda)
English, meaning 'wealthy and happy'.

Edelmira
Spanish, meaning 'admired for nobility'.

Eden
(alt. Edie, Eddie)
Hebrew, meaning 'pleasure'.

Edina
Scottish, meaning 'from Edinburgh'.

Edith
(alt. Edyth)
English, meaning 'prosperity through battle'.

Edna
Hebrew, meaning 'enjoyment'.

E

Edrea
English, meaning 'wealthy and powerful'.

Edwina
English, meaning 'wealthy friend'.

Effie
Greek, meaning 'pleasant speech'.

Eglantine
French, from the shrub of the same name.

Eileen
(alt. Eibhlín)
Irish, meaning 'shining and brilliant'.

Ekaterina
(alt. Ekaterini)
Slavic, meaning 'pure'.

Elaine
(alt. Elaina, Elayne)
French, meaning 'bright, shining light'.

Elba
Italian, from the island of the same name.

Elberta
English, meaning 'high-born'.

Eldora
Spanish, meaning 'covered with gold'.

Eleanor
(alt. Elana, Elanor, Eleanora, Eleanore, Elena, Eleni, Elenor, Elenora, Elina, Elinor, Elinore)
Greek, meaning 'light'.

Electra
(alt. Elektra)
Greek, meaning 'shining', also from the myth.

Elfrida
(alt. Elfrieda)
English, meaning 'elf power'.

Eliane
Hebrew, meaning 'Jehovah is God'.

Elissa
(alt. Elise)
French, meaning 'pledged to God'.

Eliza
(alt. Elisha, Elise)
Hebrew, meaning 'pledged to God'.

Elizabeth
(alt. Elisabet, Elisabeth, Elizabella, Elsbeth, Elspeth)
Hebrew, meaning 'pledged to God'. The name of the Queen of England.

Elke
German, meaning 'nobility'.

Ella
German, meaning 'completely'.

Elle
(alt. Ellie)
French, meaning 'she'.

Ellen
(alt. Elin, Eline, Ellyn)
Greek, meaning 'shining'.

Ellice
(alt. Elyse)
Greek, meaning 'the Lord is God'.

Elma
(alt. Elna)
Latin, meaning 'soul'.

Elmira
Arabic, meaning 'aristocratic lady'.

Elodie
French, meaning 'marsh flower'.

Eloise
(alt. Elois, Eloisa, Elouise)
French, meaning 'renowned in battle'.

Elsa
(alt. Else, Elsie)
Hebrew, meaning 'pledged to God'.

Elula
Hebrew, meaning 'August'.

Elva
Irish, meaning 'noble'.

Elvina
English, meaning 'noble friend'.

Elvira
(alt. Elvera)
Spanish, from the place of the same name.

Ember
(alt. Embry)
English, meaning 'spark'.

Emeline
German, meaning 'industrious'.

Emerald
English, meaning 'green gemstone'.

Emery
(alt. Emory)
German, meaning 'ruler of work'.

Emilia
Latin, meaning 'rival, eager'.

Emily
(alt. Emelie, Emilee, Emilie, Emlyn)
Latin, meaning 'rival, eager'.

Emma
(alt. Emme, Emmi, Emmie, Emmy)
German, meaning 'embraces everything'.

E

Emmanuelle
Hebrew, meaning 'God is among us'.

Emmeline
(alt. Emmelina)
German, meaning 'embraces everything'.

Ena
Shortened form of Georgina, meaning 'farmer'.

Enid
(alt. Eneida)
Welsh, meaning 'life spirit'.

Enola
Native American, meaning 'solitary'.

Enya
Irish Gaelic, meaning 'fire'. Made popular by Irish singer Enya.

Erica
(alt. Ericka, Erika)
Scandinavian, meaning 'ruler forever'.

Erin
(alt. Eryn)
Irish Gaelic, meaning 'from the isle to the west'.

Eris
Greek, from the mythological heroine of the same name.

Erlinda
Hebrew, meaning 'spirited'.

Erma
German, meaning 'universal'.

Ermine
French, meaning 'weasel'.

Erna
English, meaning 'sincere'.

Ernestine
(alt. Ernestina)
English, meaning 'sincere'.

Esme
French, meaning 'esteemed'.

Esmeralda
Spanish, meaning 'emerald'.

Esperanza
Spanish, meaning 'hope'.

Estelle
(alt. Estela, Estell, Estella)
French, meaning 'star'.

Esther
(alt. Esta, Ester, Etha, Ethna, Ethne)
Persian, meaning 'star'. Key biblical character in the Book of Esther.

Eternity
Latin, meaning 'forever'.

E

Ethel
(alt. Ethyl)
English, meaning 'noble'.

Etta
(alt. Etter, Ettie)
Shortened form of Henrietta, meaning 'ruler of the house'.

Eudora
Greek, meaning 'generous gift'.

Eugenia
(alt. Eugenie)
Greek, meaning 'well born'.

Eulalia
(alt. Eula, Eulah, Eulalie)
Greek, meaning 'sweet-speaking'.

Eunice
Greek, meaning 'victorious'.

Euphemia
Greek, meaning ' favorable speech'.

Eva
Hebrew, meaning 'life'.
Associated with the first woman to walk the earth.

Evadne
Greek, meaning 'pleasing one'.

Evangeline
(alt. Evangelina)
Greek, meaning 'good news'.

Evanthe
Greek, meaning 'good flower'.

Eve
(alt. Evie)
Hebrew, meaning 'life'.
Associated with the first woman to walk the earth.

Evelina
(alt. Evelia)
German, meaning 'hazelnut'.

Evelyn
(alt. Evalyn, Evelin, Eveline, Evelyne)
German, meaning 'hazelnut'.

Everly
(alt. Everleigh, Everley)
English, meaning 'grazing meadow'.

Evette
French, meaning 'yew wood'.

Evonne
(alt. Evon)
French, meaning 'yew wood'.

F Girls' names

Fabia
(alt. *Fabiana, Fabienne, Fabiola, Fabriana*)
Latin, meaning 'from the Fabian clan'.

Fabrizia
Italian, meaning 'works with hands'.

Faith
English, meaning 'loyalty'.

Faiza
Arabic, meaning 'victorious'.

Fallon
Irish Gaelic, meaning 'descended from a ruler'.

Fanny
(alt. *Fannie*)
Latin, meaning 'from France'.

Farica
German, meaning 'peaceful ruler'.

Farrah
English, meaning 'lovely and pleasant'. Became popular after actress Farrah Fawcett.

Fatima
Arabic, meaning 'baby's nurse'.

Faustine
Latin, meaning 'fortunate'.

Fawn
French, meaning 'young deer'.

Fay
(alt. *Fae, Faye*)
French, meaning 'fairy'.

Felicia
(alt. *Felecia, Felice, Felicita, Felisha*)
Latin, meaning 'lucky and happy'.

Felicity
Latin, meaning 'fortunate'.

Fenella
Irish Gaelic, meaning 'white shoulder'.

Fenia
Scandinavian, from the mythological giantess of the same name.

Fern
(alt. Ferne, Ferrin)
English, from the plant of the same name.

Fernanda
German, meaning 'peace and courage'.

Ffion
(alt. Fion)
Irish Gaelic, meaning 'fair and pale'.

Fia
Italian, meaning 'flame'.

Fifi
Hebrew, meaning 'Jehovah increases'.

Filomena
Greek, meaning 'loved one'.

Finlay
(alt. Finley)
Irish Gaelic, meaning 'fair-headed courageous one'.

Finola
(alt. Fionnula)
Irish Gaelic, meaning 'fair shoulder'.

Fiona
(alt. Fiora)
Irish Gaelic, meaning 'fair and pale'.

Flanna
(alt. Flannery)
Irish Gaelic, meaning 'russet hair'.

Flavia
Latin, meaning 'yellow hair'.

Fleur
(alt. Flor)
French, meaning 'flower'.

Old name, new fashion?

Bella
Carolyn
Clara
Dorothy
Emmeline
Hazel
Matilda
Nora
Penelope
Rosalie

Flo
(alt. Florrie, Flossie, Floy)
Shortened form of Florence, meaning 'in bloom'.

Flora
Latin, meaning 'flower'.

Florence
(alt. Florencia, Florene, Florine)
Latin, meaning 'in bloom'.

Florida
Latin, meaning 'flowery'. Also the American state.

Frances
(alt. Fanny, Fran, Francine, Francis, Frankie, Frannie, Franny)
Latin, meaning 'from France'.

Francesca
(alt. Franchesca, Francisca)
Latin, meaning 'from France'.

Freda
(alt. Freida, Frida, Frieda)
German, meaning 'peaceful'.

Frederica
German, meaning 'peaceful ruler'.

Fuchsia
German, from the flower of the same name.

Names of First Ladies

Barbara (Bush)
Edith (Roosevelt)
Elizabeth (Ford)
Grace (Coolidge)
Hillary (Clinton)
Jacqueline (Kennedy)
Martha (Washington)
Mary (Lincoln)
Michelle (Obama)
Nancy (Reagan)

F

G

Girls' names

Gabrielle
(alt. Gabbi, Gabby, Gabriel, Gabriela, Gabriella)
Hebrew, meaning 'heroine of God'.

Gaia
(alt. Gaea)
Greek, meaning 'the earth'.

Gail
(alt. Gale, Gayla, Gayle)
Hebrew, meaning 'my father rejoices'.

Gala
French, meaning 'festive merrymaking'.

Galiena
German, meaning 'high one'.

Galina
Russian, meaning 'shining brightly'.

Garnet
(alt. Garnett)
English, meaning 'red gemstone'.

Gay
(alt. Gaye)
French, meaning 'glad and lighthearted'.

Gaynor
Welsh, meaning 'white and smooth'.

Gemini
Greek, meaning 'twin'. The third astrological sign in the Zodiac.

Gemma
Italian, meaning 'precious stone'.

Gene
Greek, meaning 'well born'.

Genesis

Greek, meaning 'beginning'. The first book of the Old Testament.

Geneva

(alt. Genevra)
French, meaning 'juniper tree'.

Genevieve

(alt. Genie)
German, meaning 'white wave'.

Georgette

French, meaning 'farmer'.

Georgia

(alt. Georgie)
Latin, meaning 'farmer'.

Georgina

(alt. Georgene, Georgiana, Georgianna, Georgine, Giorgina)
Latin, meaning 'farmer'.

Geraldine

German, meaning 'spear ruler'.

Gerda

Nordic, meaning 'shelter'.

Geri

(alt. Gerri, Gerry)
Shortened form of Geraldine, meaning 'spear ruler'.

Names from ancient Rome

Agrippina
Antonia
Claudia
Drusilla
Honorata
Hortensia
Narcissa
Romana
Tatiana
Valeria

Germaine

French, meaning 'from Germany'.

Gertrude

(alt. Gertie)
German, meaning 'strength of a spear'.

Gia

(alt. Ghia)
Italian, meaning 'God is gracious'.

Gianina

(alt. Giana)
Hebrew, meaning 'God's graciousness'.

G

Gigi
(alt. Giget)
Shortened form of Georgina, meaning 'farmer'.

Gilda
English, meaning 'gilded'.

Gilia
Hebrew, meaning 'joy of the Lord'.

Gillian
Latin, meaning 'youthful'.

Gina
(alt. Geena, Gena)
Shortened form of Regina, meaning 'queen'.

Ginger
Latin, from the root of the same name.

Ginny
Shortened form of Virginia, meaning 'virgin'.

Giovanna
Italian, meaning 'God is gracious'.

Giselle
(alt. Gisela, Gisele, Giselle, Gisselle)
German, meaning 'pledge'.

Gita
(alt. Geeta)
Sanskrit, meaning 'song'. The Bhagavad Gita is a important part of Hindu Scripture, and is often simply known as the Gita.

Giulia
(alt. Giuliana)
Italian, meaning 'youthful'.

Gladys
(alt. Gladyce)
Welsh, meaning 'lame'.

Glenda
Welsh, meaning 'fair and good'.

Glenna
(alt. Glennie)
Irish Gaelic, meaning 'glen'.

Gloria
(alt. Glory)
Latin, meaning 'glory'.

Glynda
(alt. Glinda)
Welsh, meaning 'fair'.

Glynis
Welsh, meaning 'small glen'.

Golda
(alt. Goldia, Goldie)
English, meaning 'gold'.

G

Grace
(alt. Graça, Gracie, Gracin, Grayce)
Latin, meaning 'grace'.

Grainne
(alt. Grania)
Irish Gaelic, meaning 'love'.

Gratia
(alt. Grasia)
Latin, meaning 'blessing'.

Greer
(alt. Grier)
Latin, meaning 'alert and watchful'.

Gregoria
Latin, meaning 'alert'.

Greta
(alt. Gretel)
Greek, meaning 'pearl'.

Gretchen
German, meaning 'pearl'.

Griselda
(alt. Griselle)
German, meaning 'gray fighting maid'.

Gudrun
Scandinavian, meaning 'battle'.

Guinevere
Welsh, meaning 'white and smooth'. The legendary Queen consort of King Arthur.

Gwenda
Welsh, meaning 'fair and good'.

Gwendolyn
(alt. Gwen, Gwendolen, Gwenel)
Welsh, meaning 'fair bow'.

Gwyneth
(alt. Gwynneth, Gwynyth)
Welsh, meaning 'happiness'.

Gwynn
(alt. Gwyn)
Welsh, meaning 'fair blessed'.

Gypsy
English, meaning 'of the Roman tribe'.

Names from ancient Greece

Alexandra
Apollonia
Corinna
Irene
Lysandra
Melaina
Pelagia
Sophia
Xenia
Zenobia

G

250

Popular Irish names for boys and girls

Aidan	Eileen
Aisling	Kieran
Connor	Liam
Declan	Niamh
Deidre	Siobhan

H Girls' names

Hadassah
Hebrew, meaning
'myrtle tree'.

Hadley
English, meaning 'heather
meadow'.

Hadria
Latin, meaning 'from Hadria'.

Hala
Arabic, meaning 'halo'.

Haley
*(alt. Hailee, Hailey, Hailie,
Haleigh, Hali, Halie)*
English, meaning 'hay
meadow'.

Halima
(alt. Halina)
Arabic, meaning 'gentle'.

Hallie
(alt. Halle, Halley)
German, meaning 'ruler of the
home or estate'.

Hannah
(alt. Haana, Hana, Hanna)
Hebrew, meaning 'grace'.

Harley
(alt. Harlene)
English, meaning 'the long
field'.

Harlow
English, meaning 'army hill'.
Associated with actress Jean
Harlow.

Harmony
Latin, meaning 'harmony'.

Harper
English, meaning 'minstrel'.

Harriet
(alt. Harriett, Harriette, Hattie)
German, meaning 'ruler of the home or estate'.

Haven
English, meaning 'a place of sanctuary'.

Hayden
Old English, meaning 'hedged valley'.

Hayley
(alt. Haylee, Hayleigh, Haylie)
English, meaning 'hay meadow'.

Hazel
(alt. Hazle)
English, from the tree of the same name.

Heather
English, from the flower of the same name.

Heaven
English, meaning 'everlasting bliss'.

Hedda
German, meaning 'warfare'.

Hedwig
German, meaning 'warfare and strife'. Harry Potter's constant owl companion.

Heidi
(alt. Heidy)
German, meaning 'nobility'.

Helen
(alt. Halen, Helena, Helene, Hellen)
Greek, meaning 'light'. In Greek mythology Helen of Troy was considered to be the most beautiful woman in the world.

Helga
German, meaning 'holy and sacred'.

Heloise
French, meaning 'renowned in war'.

Henrietta
(alt. Henriette)
German, meaning 'ruler of the house'.

Hephzibah
Hebrew, meaning 'my delight is in her'.

Hera
Greek, meaning 'queen'.

Hermia
(alt. Hermina, Hermine, Herminia)
Greek, meaning 'messenger'.

Names with positive meanings

Belle (Beautiful)
Blythe (Carefree)
Felicity (Happy)
Lakshmi (Good)
Lucy (Light)
Millicent (Brave)
Mira (Wonderful)
Rinah (Joyful)
Sunny (Sunshine)
Yoko (Positive)

Hermione
Greek, meaning 'earthly'. Harry Potter's closest (and smartest) female friend.

Hero
Greek, meaning 'brave one of the people'.

Hertha
English, meaning 'earth'.

Hesper
(alt. Hesperia)
Greek, meaning 'evening star'.

Hester
(alt. Hestia)
Greek, meaning 'star'.

Hilary
(alt. Hillary)
Greek, meaning 'cheerful and happy'.

Hilda
(alt. Hildur)
German, meaning 'battle woman'.

Hildegarde
(alt. Hildegard)
German, meaning 'battle stronghold'.

Hildred
German, meaning 'battle counsellor'.

Hilma
German, meaning 'helmet'.

Hollis
English, meaning 'near the holly bushes'.

Holly
(alt. Holli, Hollie)
English, from the tree of the same name.

Honey
English, meaning 'honey'.

Honor
(alt. Honora, Honoria, Honour)
Latin, meaning 'woman of honor'.

Hope
English, meaning 'hope'.

Hortense
(alt. Hortencia, Hortensia)
Latin, meaning 'of the garden'. Also the name of Napoleon Bonaparte's mother.

Hulda
German, meaning 'loved one'.

Hyacinth
Greek, from the flower of the same name.

I Girls' names

Iantha
Greek, meaning 'purple flower'.

Ida
(alt. Idell, Idella)
English, meaning 'prosperous'. Ida B. Wells was a prominent African American civil rights activist and journalist.

Idona
Nordic, meaning 'renewal'.

Ignacia
Latin, meaning 'ardent'.

Ila
French, meaning 'island'.

Ilana
Hebrew, meaning 'tree'.

Ilaria
Italian, meaning 'cheerful'.

Ilene
American, meaning 'light'.

Iliana
(alt. Ileana)
Greek, meaning 'Trojan'.

Ilona
Hungarian, meaning 'light'.

Ilsa
German, meaning 'pledged to God'.

Ima
German, meaning 'embraces everything'.

Iman
Arabic, meaning 'faith'.

Imelda
German, meaning 'all-consuming fight'.

I

Imogen
(alt. Imogene)
Latin, meaning 'last-born'.

Ina
Latin, meaning 'to make feminine'.

Inaya
Arabic, meaning 'taking care'.

India
(alt. Indie)
Hindi, from the country of the same name.

Indiana
Latin, meaning 'from India'. Also the midwestern state.

Indigo
Greek, meaning 'deep blue dye'.

Indira
(alt. Inira)
Sanskrit, meaning 'beauty'.

Inez
(alt. Ines)
Spanish, meaning 'pure'.

Inga
(alt. Inge, Ingeborg, Inger)
Scandinavian, meaning 'guarded by Ing'.

Ingrid
Scandinavian, meaning 'beautiful'.

Io
(alt. Eye)
Greek, from the mythological heroine of the same name.

Ioanna
Greek, meaning 'grace'.

Iola
(alt. Iole)
Greek, meaning 'cloud of dawn'.

Iolanthe
Greek, meaning 'violet flower'. Also the name of the comic opera by Gilbert and Sullivan.

Iona
Greek, from the island of the same name.

Ione
Greek, meaning 'violet'.

Iphigenia
Greek, meaning 'sacrifice'.

Ira
(alt. Iva)
Hebrew, meaning 'watchful'.

Irene
(alt. Irelyn, Irena, Irina, Irini)
Greek, meaning 'peace'.

Iris
Greek, meaning 'rainbow'.

Irma
German, meaning 'universal'.

Isabel
(alt. *Isabela, Isabell, Isabella, Isabelle, Isobel, Izabella, Izabelle*)
Spanish, meaning 'pledged to God'.

Isadora
Latin, meaning 'gift of Isis'.

Ishana
Hindi, meaning 'desire'.

Isis
Egyptian, from the goddess of the same name. She was worshipped as the ideal mother and wife, and the goddess of nature and magic.

Isla
(alt. *Isa, Isela, Isley*)
Scottish Gaelic, meaning 'river'.

Isolde
Welsh, meaning 'fair lady'.

Ivana
Slavic, meaning 'Jehovah is gracious'.

Ivette
Variation of Yvette, meaning 'yew wood'.

Ivonne
Variation of Yvonne, meaning 'yew wood'.

Ivory
Latin, meaning 'white as elephant tusks'.

Ivy
English, from the plant of the same name. Recently surged in popularity thanks to Beyoncé and Jay-Z's name choice for their daughter Blue Ivy.

Ixia
South African, from the flower of the same name.

Boys' names for girls (female spellings)

Ashley
Billie
Casey
Charlie
Elliott
Geri
Jamie
Jordan
Leigh
Toni

I

J Girls' names

Jacinda
(alt. Jacinta)
Spanish, meaning 'hyacinth'.

Jackie
(alt. Jacky, Jacque, Jacqui)
Shortened form of Jacqueline,
meaning 'he who supplants'.

Jacqueline
(alt. Jacalyn, Jacklyn, Jaclyn,
Jacquelin, Jacquelyn, Jacquline,
Jaquelin, Jaqueline)
French, meaning 'he who
supplants'.

Jade
(alt. Jada, Jaida, Jayda, Jayde)
Spanish, meaning 'green stone'.

Jaden
(alt. Jadyn, Jaiden, Jayden)
Contraction of Jade and
Hayden, meaning 'green
hedged valley'.

Jael
Hebrew, meaning 'mountain
goat'.

Jaime
(alt. Jaima, Jaimie, Jami,
Jamie)
Spanish, meaning 'he who
supplants'. J'aime is also French
for 'I love'.

Jamila
Arabic, meaning 'lovely'.

Jan
(alt. Joana, Jana, Jann, Janna)
Hebrew, meaning 'the Lord is
gracious'.

Janae
(alt. Janay)
American, meaning 'the Lord is
gracious'.

Jane
(alt. Jayne)
Feminine form of John,
meaning 'the Lord is gracious'.

Janelle
(alt. Janel, Janell, Jenelle)
American, meaning 'the Lord is
gracious'.

Janet
(alt. Janette)
Scottish, meaning 'the Lord is
gracious'.

Janice
(alt. Janis)
American, meaning 'the Lord is
gracious'.

Janie
(alt. Janey, Janney, Jannie)
Shortened form of Janet,
meaning 'the Lord is gracious'.

Janine
(alt. Janeen)
English, meaning 'the Lord is
gracious'.

Janoah
(alt. Janiya, Janiyah)
Hebrew, meaning 'quiet and
calm'.

January
Latin, meaning 'the first
month'.

Jasmine
(alt. Jasmin, Jazim, Jazmine)
Persian, meaning 'jasmine
flower'. Also the name of the
princess in Disney's Aladdin.

Jay
Latin, meaning 'jaybird'.

Jayna
Sanskrit, meaning 'bringer of
victory'.

Jean
(alt. Jeane, Jeanie, Jeanne,
Jeannie)
Scottish, meaning 'the Lord is
gracious'.

Jeana
(alt. Jeanna)
Latin, meaning 'queen'.

Jeanette
(alt. Jeannette, Janette)
French, meaning 'the Lord is
gracious'.

Jeanine
(alt. Jeannine)
Latin, meaning 'the Lord is
gracious'.

Jemima
Hebrew, meaning 'dove'.

Jemma
English variant of Gemma,
meaning 'precious stone'.

J

Jena
Arabic, meaning 'little bird'.

Jenna
Hebrew, meaning 'the Lord is gracious'.

Jennifer
(alt. Jenifer, Jennie, Jenny)
Welsh, meaning 'white and smooth'. One of the most consistently popular names for baby girls.

Jerrie
(alt. Jeri, Jerri, Jerrie, Jerry)
German, meaning 'spear ruler'.

Jerusha
Hebrew, meaning 'married'.

Jeryl
English, meaning 'spear ruler'.

Flower names

Daisy
Flora
Heather
Hyacinth
Iris
Lily
Poppy
Primrose
Rose
Violet

Jessa
Shortened form of Jessica, meaning 'He sees'.

Jessamy
(alt. Jessame, Jessamine, Jessamyn)
Persian, meaning 'jasmine flower'.

Jessica
(alt. Jesica, Jessika)
Hebrew, meaning 'He sees'.

Jessie
(alt. Jesse, Jessi, Jessy)
Shortened form of Jessica, meaning 'He sees'.

Jesusa
Spanish, meaning 'mother of the Lord'.

Jette
(alt. Jetta, Jettie)
Danish, meaning 'black as coal'.

Jewel
(alt. Jewell)
French, meaning 'delight'. Associated with singer songwriter Jewel.

Jezebel
(alt. Jezabel, Jezabelle)
Hebrew, meaning 'pure and virginal'.

J

Jill
Latin, meaning 'youthful'.

Jillian
Latin, meaning 'youthful'.

Jimena
Spanish, meaning 'heard'.

Joan
Hebrew, meaning 'the Lord is gracious'.

Joanna
(alt. Jo, Joana, Joanie, Joann, Joanne, Johanna, Joni)
Hebrew, meaning 'the Lord is gracious'.

Jocasta
Italian, meaning 'lighthearted'.

Jocelyn
(alt. Jauslyn, Jocelyne, Joscelin, Joslyn)
German, meaning 'cheerful'.

Jody
(alt. Jodee, Jodi, Jodie)
Shortened form of Judith, meaning 'Jewish'.

Joelle
(alt. Joela)
Hebrew, meaning 'Jehovah is the Lord'.

Joie
French, meaning 'joy'.

Jolene
Contraction of Joanna and Darlene, meaning 'gracious darling'.

Jolie
(alt. Joely)
French, meaning 'pretty'.

Jonisa
(alt. Jonisha)
Hebrew and French, meaning 'God is gracious'.

Jordan
(alt. Jordana, Jordin, Jordyn)
Hebrew, meaning 'descend'.

Josephine
(alt. Josefina, Josephina)
Hebrew, meaning 'Jehovah increases'.

Josie
(alt. Joss, Jossie)
Shortened form of Josephine, meaning 'Jehovah increases'.

Jovita
(alt. Jovie)
Latin, meaning 'made glad'.

Joy
Latin, meaning 'joy'.

Joyce
Latin, meaning 'joyous'.

Juanita
(alt. Juana)
Spanish, meaning 'the Lord is gracious'.

Jubilee
Hebrew, meaning 'ram's horn' or 'special anniversary'.

Judith
(alt. Judit)
Hebrew, meaning 'Jewish'.

Judy
(alt. Judi, Judie)
Shortened form of Judith, Hebrew meaning 'Jewish'.

Jules
French, meaning 'Jove's child'.

Julia
(alt. Juli, Julie)
Latin, meaning 'youthful'.

Julianne
(alt. Juliana, Juliann, Julianne)
Latin, meaning 'youthful'.

Juliet
(alt. Joliet, Juliette)
Latin, meaning 'youthful'.

June
(alt. Juna)
Latin, after the month of the same name.

Juniper
Dutch, from the shrub of the same name.

Juno
(alt. Juneau)
Latin, meaning 'queen of heaven'. Juno was an ancient Roman goddess.

Justice
English, meaning 'to deliver what is just'.

Justine
(alt. Justina)
Latin, meaning 'fair and righteous'.

Jorgina
Dutch, meaning 'farmer'.

J

K Girls' names

Kadenza
(alt. Kadence)
Latin, meaning 'with rhythm'.

Kaitlin
(alt. Kaitlyn)
Greek, meaning 'pure'.

Kala
(alt. Kaela, Kaiala, Kaila)
Sanskrit, meaning 'black one'.

Kali
(alt. Kailey, Kaleigh, Kaley, Kalie, Kalli, Kally, Kaylee, Kayleigh)
Sanskrit, meaning 'black one'.

Kalila
Arabic, meaning 'beloved'.

Kalina
Slavic, meaning 'flower'.

Kalliope
(alt. Calliope)
Greek, meaning 'beautiful voice'. From the muse of the same name.

Kallista
Greek, meaning 'most beautiful'.

Kama
Sanskrit, meaning 'love'.

Kami
Japanese, meaning 'lord'.

Kamilla
(alt. Kamilah)
Slavic, meaning 'serving girl'.

Kana
Hawaiian, from the demi-god of the same name.

Place names

Ailsa
Alexandria
Brittany
Eden
India
Lydia
Martinique
Normandie
Paris
Skye

Kandace
(alt. Kandice)
Latin, meaning 'glowing white'.

Kandy
(alt. Kandi)
Shortened form of Kandace, meaning 'glowing white'.

Kara
Latin, meaning 'dear one'.

Karen
(alt. Karan, Karin, Karina, Karon, Karren)
Greek, meaning 'pure'.

Kari
(alt. Karie, Karri, Karrie)
Shortened form of Karen, meaning 'pure'.

Karimah
Arabic, meaning 'giving'.

Karissa
(alt. Carissa, Korissa)
Greek, meaning 'very dear'.

Karishma
Sanskrit, meaning 'miracle'.

Karla
(alt. Karlyn)
German, meaning 'man'.

Karly
(alt. Karlee, Karley, Karli)
German, meaning 'free man'.

Karma
Hindi, meaning 'destiny'.

Karol
(alt. Karolina, Karolyn)
Slavic, meaning 'little and womanly'.

Kasey
(alt. Kacey, Kaci, Kacie, Kacy, Kasie, Kassie)
Irish Gaelic, meaning 'alert and watchful'.

Kassandra
Greek, meaning 'she who entangles men'.

Katarina
(alt. Katarine, Katerina, Katharina)
Greek, meaning 'pure'.

K

Kate
(alt. Kat, Katie, Kathi, Kathie, Kathy, Kati, Katy)
Shortened form of Katherine, meaning 'pure'.

Katelyn
(alt. Katelin, Katelynn, Katlin, Katlyn)
Greek, meaning 'pure'.

Katherine
(alt. Katharine, Kathrine, Kathryn)
Greek, meaning 'pure'.

Kathleen
(alt. Kathlyn)
Greek, meaning 'pure'.

Katniss
American, meaning 'arrowhead plant'.

Katrina
(alt. Katina)
Greek, meaning 'pure'.

Katya
(alt. Katyea)
Greek, meaning 'pure'.

Kay
(alt. Kaye)
Shortened form of Katherine, meaning 'pure'.

Kaya
Sanskrit, meaning 'nature', or Turkish, meaning 'rock'.

Kayla
(alt. Kaylah)
Greek, meaning 'pure'.

Kayley
(alt. Kayley, Kayli, Kaylin)
American, meaning 'pure'.

Keeley
(alt. Keely)
Irish, meaning 'battle maid'.

Keila
Hebrew, meaning 'citadel'.

Keira
Irish Gaelic, meaning 'dark'.

Keisha
(alt. Keesha)
Arabic, meaning 'woman'.

Kelis
American, meaning 'beautiful'. Popularized by the pop singer of the same name.

Kelly
(alt. Keli, Kelley, Kelli, Kellie)
Irish Gaelic, meaning 'battle maid'.

Kelsey
(alt. Kelcie, Kelsea, Kelsi, Kelsie)
English, meaning 'island'.

Kendall
(alt. Kendal)
English, meaning 'the valley of the Kent'.

Kendra
English, meaning 'knowing'.

Kenna
Irish Gaelic, meaning 'handsome'.

Kennedy
(alt. Kenadee, Kennedi)
Irish Gaelic, meaning 'helmet head'.

Kenya
African, from the country of the same name.

Kenzie
Shortened form of Mackenzie, meaning 'son of the wise ruler'.

Kerensa
Cornish, meaning 'love'.

Kerrigan
Irish, meaning 'black haired'.

Kerry
(alt. Keri, Kerri, Kerrie)
Irish, from the county of the same name.

Khadijah
(alt. Khadejah)
Arabic, meaning 'premature baby'.

Kiana
(alt. Kia, Kiana)
American, meaning 'fibre'.

Kiara
Italian, meaning 'light'.

Kiki
Spanish, meaning 'home ruler'.

Kim
Shortened form of Kimberly, meaning 'royal forest'.

Kimberly
(alt. Kimberleigh, Kimberley)
Old English, meaning 'royal forest'. Also a town in South Africa.

Kingsley
(alt. Kinsley)
English, meaning 'king's meadow'.

Kinsey
English, meaning 'king's victory'.

Kira
Greek, meaning 'lady'.

K

Long names

Alexandria
Bernadette
Christabelle
Constantine
Evangeline
Gabrielle
Henrietta
Jacqueline
Marguerite
Wilhelmina

Kiri
Maori, meaning 'tree bark'.

Kirsten
(alt. Kirstin)
Scandinavian, meaning 'Christian'.

Kirstie
(alt. Kirsty)
Shortened form of Kirsten, meaning 'Christian'.

Kitty
(alt. Kittie)
Shortened form of Katherine, meaning 'pure'.

Kizzy
Hebrew, meaning the plant 'cassia'.

Klara
Hungarian, meaning 'bright'.

Komal
Hindi, meaning 'soft and tender'.

Konstantina
Latin, meaning 'steadfast'.

Kora
(alt. Kori)
Greek, meaning 'maiden'.

Kris
(alt. Krista, Kristi, Kristie, Kristy)
Shortened form of Kristen, meaning 'Christian'.

Kristen
(alt. Kristan, Kristin, Kristine)
Greek, meaning 'Christian'.

Krystal
(alt. Kristal, Kristel)
Greek, meaning 'ice'.

Kwanza
(alt. Kwanzaa)
African, meaning 'beginning'. Also the name of the week-long festival in December and January.

Kyla
(alt. Kya, Kylah, Kyle)
Scottish, meaning 'narrow spit of land'.

Kylie
(alt. Kiley, Kylee)
Irish Gaelic, meaning 'graceful'.

Kyra
Greek, meaning 'lady'.

Kyrie
Greek, meaning 'the Lord'.

Short names

Bea
Bo
Fay
Jan
Jo
Kay
Kim
May
Mia
Val

L Girls' names

Lacey
(alt. Laci, Lacie, Lacy)
French, from the town of the same name.

Ladonna
Italian, meaning 'lady'.

Lady
English, meaning 'bread kneader'.

Laila
(alt. Layla, Leila, Lejla, Lela, Lelah, Lelia)
Arabic, meaning 'night'.

Lainey
(alt. Laine, Laney)
French, meaning 'bright light'.

Lakeisha
(alt. Lakeshia)
American, meaning 'woman'.

Lakshmi
(alt. Laxmi)
Sanskrit, meaning 'good omen'.

Lana
Greek, meaning 'light'.

Lani
(alt. Lanie)
Hawaiian, meaning 'sky'.

Lara
Latin, meaning 'famous'.

Laraine
French, meaning 'from Lorraine'.

Larissa
(alt. Larisa)
Greek, meaning 'light-hearted'.

Lark
(alt. Larkin)
English, meaning 'playful songbird'.

Larsen
Scandinavian, meaning 'son of Lars'.

Latifa
Arabic, meaning 'gentle and pleasant'.

Latika
(alt. Lotika)
Hindi, meaning 'a plant'.

Latisha
Latin, meaning 'happiness'.

Latona
(alt. Latonia)
Roman, from the mythological heroine of the same name.

Latoya
Spanish, meaning 'victorious one'.

Latrice
(alt. Latricia)
Latin, meaning 'noble'.

Laura
(alt. Lora)
Latin, meaning 'laurel'.

Laurel
Latin, meaning 'laurel tree'.

Lauren
(alt. Lauran, Loren)
Latin, meaning 'laurel'.

Laveda
(alt. Lavada)
Latin, meaning 'cleansed'.

Lavender
Latin, from the plant of the same name.

Laverne
(alt. Lavern, Laverna)
Latin, from the goddess of the same name. Made popular by the TV sitcom *Laverne & Shirley* in the 70s.

Lavinia
(alt. Lavina)
Latin, meaning 'woman of Rome'.

Lavonne
(alt. Lavon)
French, meaning 'yew wood'.

Leah
(alt. Lea, Leia)
Hebrew, meaning 'weary'.

Leandra
Greek, meaning 'lion man'.

Leanne
(alt. Leann, Leanna, Leeann)
Contraction of Lee and Ann, meaning 'meadow grace'.

Leda
Greek, meaning 'gladness'.

L

'Bad girl' names

Delilah
Desdemona
Jezebel
Lilith
Pandora
Roxy
Salome
Scarlett
Tallulah
Trixie

Lee
(alt. Leigh)
English, meaning 'pasture or meadow'.

Leilani
Hawaiian, meaning 'flower from heaven'.

Leith
Scottish Gaelic, meaning 'broad river'.

Lena
(alt. Leena, Lina)
Latin, meaning 'light'. Currently made popular by actress and filmmaker Lena Dunham.

Lenna
(alt. Lennie)
German, meaning 'lion's strength'.

Léonie
(alt. Leona, Leone)
Latin, meaning 'lion'.

Leonora
(alt. Lenora, Lenore, Leonor, Leonore, Leora)
Greek, meaning 'light'.

Leslie
(alt. Leslee, Lesley)
Scottish Gaelic, meaning 'the gray castle'.

Leta
Latin, meaning 'glad and joyful'.

Letha
Greek, meaning 'forgetfulness'.

Letitia
(alt. Leticia, Lettice, Lettie)
Latin, meaning 'joy and gladness'.

Lexia
(alt. Lexi, Lexie)
Greek, meaning 'defender of mankind'.

Lia
Italian, meaning 'bringer of the gospel'.

Liana
French, meaning 'to twine around'.

Libby
(alt. Libbie)
Shortened form of Elizabeth, meaning 'pledged to God'.

Liberty
English, meaning 'freedom'.

Lida
Slavic, meaning 'loved by the people'.

Liese
(alt. Liesel, Liesl)
German, meaning 'pledged to God'.

Lila
(alt. Lilah)
Arabic, meaning 'night'.

Lilac
Latin, from the flower of the same name.

Lilia
(alt. Lilias)
Scottish, meaning 'lily'.

Lilith
Arabic, meaning 'ghost'. In Jewish mythology Lilith was thought to be a female demon.

Lillian
(alt. Lilian, Liliana, Lilla, Lillianna)
Latin, meaning 'lily'.

Lily
(alt. Lili, Lillie, Lilly)
Latin, from the flower of the same name.

Linda
(alt. Lynda)
Spanish, meaning 'pretty'.

Linden
(alt. Lindie, Lindy)
European, from the tree of the same name.

Lindsay
(alt. Lindsey, Linsey)
English, meaning 'island of linden trees'.

Linette
Welsh, meaning 'idol'.

Linnea
(alt. Linnae, Linny)
Scandinavian, meaning 'lime or linden tree'. An extremely popular name for baby girls in Sweden.

Liora
(alt. Lior)
Hebrew, meaning 'I have a light'.

L

Lisa
(alt. *Leesa, Lise, Liza*)
Hebrew, meaning 'pledged to God'.

Lish
Shortened form of Elisha, meaning 'my God is salvation'.

Lissa
Greek, meaning 'bee'.

Lissandra
(alt. *Lisandra*)
Greek, meaning 'man's defender'.

Liv
Nordic, meaning 'defence'.

Great female singers

Adele (Adkins)
Aretha (Franklin)
Billie (Holiday)
Dionne (Warwick)
Dolly (Parton)
Ella (Fitzgerald)
Gladys (Knight)
Jennifer (Hudson)
Judy (Garland)
Nina (Simone)

Livia
Latin, meaning 'olive'.

Liz
(alt. *Lizzie, Lizzy*)
Shortened form of Elizabeth, meaning 'pledged to God'.

Logan
Irish Gaelic, meaning 'small hollow'.

Lois
German, meaning 'renowned in battle'.

Lolita
(alt. *Lola*)
Spanish, meaning 'sorrows'.

Lollie
(alt. *Lollie*)
Shortened form of Lolita, meaning 'sorrows'.

Lona
Latin, meaning 'lion'.

Lorelei
(alt. *Loralai, Loralie*)
German, meaning 'dangerous rock'.

Lorenza
Latin, meaning 'from Laurentium'.

Loretta
(alt. Loreto)
Latin, meaning 'laurel'.

Lori
(alt. Laurie, Lorie, Lorri)
Latin, meaning 'laurel'.

Lorna
Scottish, from the place of the same name.

Lorraine
(alt. Loraine)
French, meaning 'from Lorraine'.

Lottie
(alt. Lotta, Lotte)
French, meaning 'little and womanly'.

Lotus
Greek, meaning 'lotus flower'.

Louise
(alt. Lou, Louie, Louisa, Luisa)
German, meaning 'renowned in battle'.

Lourdes
French, from the town of the same name.

Love
English, meaning 'love'.

Lowri
Welsh, meaning 'crowned with laurels'.

Luanne
(alt. Luann, Luanna)
German, meaning 'renowned in battle'.

Lucia
(alt. Luciana)
Italian, meaning 'light'.

Lucille
(alt. Lucile, Lucilla)
French, meaning 'light'.

Lucinda
English, meaning 'light'.

Lucretia
(alt. Lucrece)
Spanish, meaning 'light'. Important figure in Ancient Roman history.

Lucy
(alt. Lucie)
Latin, meaning 'light'.

Ludmilla
Slavic, meaning 'beloved of the people'.

Luella
(alt. Lue)
English, meaning 'renowned in battle'.

Lulu
(alt. Lula)
German, meaning 'renowned in battle'.

Luna
Latin, meaning 'moon'.

Lupita
Spanish, from the town of the same name.

Luz
Spanish, meaning 'light'.

Lydia
(alt. Lidia)
Greek, meaning 'from Lydia'.

Lynsey
(alt. Lynsea)
Variation of Lindsay, meaning 'island of linden trees'.

Lynn
(alt. Lyn, Lynna, Lynne)
Spanish, meaning 'pretty; English, meaning 'waterfall'.

Lyra
Latin, meaning 'lyre'. Lyra Balacqua is the protagonist in Philip Pullman's trilogy *His Dark Materials*.

Tennis players

Anna (Kournikova)
Billie Jean (King)
Chris (Evert)
Margaret (Smith Court)
Maria (Sharapova)
Martina (Hingis/
    Navrátilová)
Monica (Seles)
Serena (Williams)
Steffi (Graf)
Venus (Williams)

L

M Girls' names

Mab
(alt. Mabe)
Irish Gaelic, meaning 'joy'.

Mabel
(alt. Mabelle, Mable)
Latin, meaning 'loveable'.

Macaria
Spanish, meaning 'blessed'.

Mackenzie
(alt. Mackenzy)
Irish Gaelic, meaning 'son of the wise ruler'.

Macy
(alt. Macey, Maci, Macie)
French, meaning 'Matthew's estate'.

Mada
English, meaning 'from Magdala'.

Madden
(alt. Maddyn)
Irish, meaning 'little dog'.

Maddie
(alt. Maddi, Maddie, Madie)
Shortened form of Madeline, meaning 'from Magdala'.

Madeline
(alt. Madaline, Madalyn, Madeleine, Madelyn, Madilyn)
Greek, meaning 'from Magdala'.

Madge
Greek, meaning 'pearl'.
Also the nickname of singer Madonna.

Madhuri
Hindi, meaning 'sweet girl'.

Madison
(alt. Maddison, Madisen,
Madisyn)
English, meaning 'son of the
mighty warrior'.

Madonna
Latin, meaning 'my lady'.

Maeve
Irish Gaelic, meaning
'intoxicating'.

Mafalda
Spanish, meaning 'battle-
mighty'.

Magali
Greek, meaning 'pearl'.

Magdalene
(alt. Magdalen, Magdalena)
Greek, meaning 'from
Magdala'.

Maggie
Shortened form of Margaret,
meaning 'pearl'.

Magnolia
Latin, from the flower of the
same name.

Mahala
(alt. Mahalia)
Hebrew, meaning 'tender
affection'.

Maia
(alt. Maja)
Greek, meaning 'mother'.

Maida
English, meaning 'maiden'.

Maisie
(alt. Maisey, Maisy, Maizie,
Masie, Mazie)
Greek, meaning 'pearl'.

Maliyah
Hawaiian, meaning 'beloved'.

Malin
(alt. Maline)
Hebrew, meaning 'of Magda'.

Malka
Hebrew, meaning 'queen'.

Mallory
(alt. Malorie)
French, meaning 'unhappy'.

Malvina
Gaelic, meaning 'smooth
brow'.

Mamie
(alt. Mammie)
Shortened form of Margaret,
meaning 'pearl'.

Mandy
(alt. Mandie)
Shortened form of Amanda,
meaning 'much loved'.

Manisha
Sanskrit, meaning 'desire'.

Mansi
Hopi, meaning 'plucked flower'.

Manuela
Spanish, meaning 'the Lord is among us'.

Mara
Hebrew, meaning 'bitter'.

Marcela
(alt. Marceline, Marcella, Marcelle)
Latin, meaning 'war-like'.

Marcia
Latin, meaning 'war-like'.

Marcy
(alt. Marci, Marcie)
Latin, meaning 'war-like'.

Margaret
(alt. Margarete, Margaretta, Margarette, Margret)
Greek, meaning 'pearl'.

Margery
(alt. Marge, Margie, Margit, Margo, Margot, Margy)
French, meaning 'pearl'.

Marguerite
(alt. Margarita)
French, meaning 'pearl'.

Maria
(alt. Mariah)
Latin, meaning 'bitter'. One of the most popular names in Spanish cultures.

Marian
(alt. Mariam, Mariana, Marion)
French, meaning 'bitter grace'.

Marianne
(alt. Maryann, Maryanne)
French, meaning 'bitter grace'.

Maribel
American, meaning 'bitterly beautiful'.

Marie
French, meaning 'bitter'.

Mariel
(alt. Mariela, Mariella)
Dutch, meaning 'bitter'.

Marietta
(alt. Marieta)
French, meaning 'bitter'.

Marigold
English, from the flower of the same name.

Marika
Dutch, meaning 'bitter'.

Marilyn
(alt. Marilee, Marilene,
Marilynn)
English, meaning 'bitter'.
Commonly associated with
the actress and singer Marilyn
Monroe.

Marin
American, from the county of
the same name.

Marina
(alt. Marine)
Latin, meaning 'from the
sea'.

Mariposa
Spanish, meaning 'butterfly'.

Marisa
(alt. Maris, Marissa)
Latin, meaning 'of the sea'.

Marisol
Spanish, meaning 'bitter sun'.

Marjolaine
French, meaning 'marjoram'.

Marjorie
(alt. Marjory)
French, meaning 'pearl'.

Marlene
(alt. Marla, Marlen, Marlena)
Hebrew, meaning 'bitter'.

Marley
(alt. Marlee)
American, meaning 'bitter'.

Marlo
(alt. Marlowe)
American, meaning 'bitter'.

Marnie
(alt. Marney)
Scottish, meaning 'from the
sea'. Rising in prominence
thanks to the HBO show Girls.

Marseille
French, from the city of the
same name.

Marsha
English, meaning 'war-like'.

Martha
(alt. Marta)
Aramaic, meaning 'lady'.

Martina
Latin, meaning 'war-like'.

Marvel
French, meaning 'something to
wonder at'.

Mary
Hebrew, meaning 'bitter'.

Masada
Hebrew, meaning 'foundation'.

Matilda
(alt. Mathilda, Mathilde)
German, meaning 'battle-mighty'.

Mattea
Hebrew, meaning 'gift of God'.

Maude
(alt. Maud)
German, meaning 'battle-mighty'.

Maura
Irish, meaning 'bitter'.

Maureen
(alt. Maurine)
Irish, meaning 'bitter'.

Mavis
French, meaning 'thrush'.

Maxine
(alt. Maxie)
Latin, meaning 'greatest'.

May
(alt. Mae, Maya, Maye, Mayra)
Hebrew, meaning 'gift of God'.
Also the fifth month.

Mckenna
(alt. Mackenna)
Irish Gaelic, meaning 'son of the handsome one'.

Mckenzie
(alt. Mckenzy, Mikenzi)
Irish Gaelic, meaning 'son of the wise ruler'.

Medea
(alt. Meda)
Greek, meaning 'ruling'.
Important figure in Greek mythology.

Meg
Shortened form of Margaret, meaning 'pearl'.

Megan
(alt. Meagan, Meghan)
Welsh, meaning 'pearl'.

Mehitabel
Hebrew, meaning 'benefited by God'.

Mehri
Persian, meaning 'kind'.

Melanie
(alt. Melania, Melany, Melonie)
Greek, meaning 'dark-skinned'.

Melba
Australian, meaning 'from Melbourne'.

Melia
(alt. Meliah)
German, meaning 'industrious'.

285

Melina
Greek, meaning 'honey'.

Melinda
Latin, meaning 'honey'.

Melisande
French, meaning 'bee'.

Melissa
(alt. Melisa, Mellissa)
Greek, meaning 'bee'.

Melody
(alt. Melodie)
Greek, meaning 'song'.

Melvina
Celtic, meaning 'chieftain'.

Menora
Hebrew, meaning 'candlestick'.

Mercedes
Spanish, meaning 'mercies'.
Usually associated with the car company Mercedes Benz.

Mercy
English, meaning 'mercy'.

Meredith
(alt. Meridith)
Welsh, meaning 'great ruler'.

Merle
French, meaning 'blackbird'.

Merry
English, meaning 'light-hearted'.

Meryl
(alt. Merrill)
Irish Gaelic, meaning 'sea-bright'.

Meta
German, meaning 'pearl'.

Mia
Italian, meaning 'mine'.

Michaela
(alt. Makaela, Makaila, Makayla, Micaela, Mikaela, Mikaila, Mikala, Mikayla)
Hebrew, meaning 'who is like the Lord'.

Michelle
(alt. Machelle, Mechelle, Michaele, Michal, Michele)
French, meaning 'who is like the Lord'.

Mickey
(alt. Micki, Mickie)
Shortened form of Michelle, meaning 'who is like the Lord'.

Migdalia
Greek, meaning 'from Magdala'.

Mignon
French, meaning 'cute'.

Mika
(alt. Micah)
Hebrew, meaning 'who resembles God'.

Milada
Czech, meaning 'my love'.

Milagros
Spanish, meaning 'miracles'.

Milan
Italian, from the city of the same name.

Mildred
English, meaning 'gentle strength'.

Milena
Czech, meaning 'love and warmth'.

Miley
American, meaning 'smiley'. Made popular by singer and actress Miley Cyrus.

Millicent
German, meaning 'high-born power'.

Millie
(alt. Milly)
Shortened form of Millicent, meaning 'high-born power'.

Mimi
Italian, meaning 'bitter'.

Popular song names

Billie Jean ("Billie Jean", Michael Jackson)
Caroline ("Sweet Caroline", Neil Diamond)
Delilah ("Delilah", Tom Jones)
Eileen ("Come on Eileen", Dexy's Midnight Runners)
Eleanor ("Eleanor Rigby", The Beatles)
Georgia ("Georgia on My Mind", Ray Charles)
Mary ("Proud Mary", Ike and Tina Turner)
Peggy Sue ("Peggy Sue", Buddy Holly)
Roxanne ("Roxanne", The Police)
Sally ("Mustang Sally", Wilson Pickett)

Mina
(alt. Mena)
German, meaning 'love'.

Mindy
(alt. Mindi)
Latin, meaning 'honey'.

Minerva
Roman, from the goddess of the same name.

Ming
Chinese, meaning 'bright'.

Minnie
(alt. Minna)
German, meaning 'helmet'. Associated with Disney's Minnie Mouse.

Mira
Latin, meaning 'admirable'.

Mirabel
(alt. Mirabella, Mirabelle)
Latin, meaning 'wonderful'.

Miranda
(alt. Meranda)
Latin, meaning 'admirable'.

Mirella
(alt. Mireille, Mirela)
Latin, meaning 'admirable'.

Miriam
Hebrew, meaning 'bitter'.

Mirta
Spanish, meaning 'crown of thorns'.

Missy
(alt. Missie)
Shortened form of Melissa, meaning 'bee'.

Misty
(alt. Misti)
English, meaning 'mist'.

Mitzi
German, meaning 'bitter'.

Miu
Japanese, meaning 'beautiful feather'.

Moira
(alt. Maira)
Irish, meaning 'bitter'.

Molly
(alt. Mollie)
American, meaning 'bitter'.

Mona
Irish Gaelic, meaning 'aristocratic'.

Monica
(alt. Monika, Monique)
Latin, meaning 'adviser'.

Monroe
Gaelic, meaning 'mouth of the river Rotha'.

M

288

Montserrat
(alt. Monserrate)
Spanish, from the town of the same name.

Morag
Scottish, meaning 'star of the sea'.

Morgan
(alt. Morgann)
Welsh, meaning 'great and bright'.

Moriah
Hebrew, meaning 'the Lord is my teacher'.

Morwenna
Welsh, meaning 'maiden'.

Moselle
(alt. Mozell, Mozella, Mozelle)
Hebrew, meaning 'savior'.

Mulan
Chinese, meaning 'wood orchid'. Name of one of the Disney princesses.

Muriel
Irish Gaelic, meaning 'sea-bright'.

Mya
(alt. Myah)
Greek, meaning 'mother'.

Myfanwy
Welsh, meaning 'my little lovely one'.

Myra
Latin, meaning 'scented oil'.

Myrna
(alt. Mirna)
Irish Gaelic, meaning 'tender and beloved'.

Myrtle
Irish, from the shrub of the same name.

N Girls' names

Nadia
(alt. Nadya)
Russian, meaning 'hope'.

Nadine
French, meaning 'hope'.

Nahara
Aramaic, meaning 'light'.

Naima
Arabic, meaning 'water nymph'.

Nalani
Hawaiian, meaning 'serenity of the skies'.

Nancy
(alt. Nan, Nanci, Nancie, Nanna, Nannie)
Hebrew, meaning 'grace'.

Nanette
(alt. Nannette)
French, meaning 'grace'.

Naomi
(alt. Naoma, Noemi)
Hebrew, meaning 'pleasant'. A key Old Testament character.

Narcissa
Greek, meaning 'daffodil'.

Nastasia
Greek, meaning 'resurrection'.

Natalie
(alt. Natalia, Natalya, Nathalie)
Latin, meaning 'birth day'.

Natasha
(alt. Natasa)
Russian, meaning 'birth day'.

Neda
English, meaning 'wealthy'.

Nedra
English, meaning 'underground'.

Neema
Swahili, meaning 'born of prosperity'.

Neka
Native American, meaning 'goose'.

Nell
(alt. Nelda, Nell, Nella, Nellie, Nelly)
Shortened form of Eleanor, meaning 'light'.

Nemi
Italian, from the lake of the same name.

Neoma
Greek, meaning 'new moon'.

Nereida
Spanish, meaning 'sea nymph'.

Nerissa
Greek, meaning 'sea nymph'.

Nettie
(alt. Neta)
Shortened form of Henrietta, meaning 'ruler of the house'.

Neva
Spanish, meaning 'snowy'.

Nevaeh
American, meaning 'heaven' (and spelt that way backwards).

Niamh
(alt. Neve)
Irish, meaning 'brightness'.

Nicola
(alt. Nicki, Nicky, Nikki)
Greek, meaning 'victory of the people'.

Nicole
(alt. Nichol, Nichole, Nicolette, Nicolle, Nikole)
Greek, meaning 'victory of the people'.

Nidia
Spanish, meaning 'graceful'.

Nigella
Irish Gaelic, meaning 'champion'.

Nikita
Greek, meaning 'unconquered'.

Nila
Egyptian, meaning 'Nile'.

Nilda
German, meaning 'battle woman'.

Nina
Spanish, meaning 'girl'.

Nissa
Hebrew, meaning 'sign'.

Nita
Spanish, meaning 'gracious'.

Nixie
German, meaning 'water sprite'.

Noel
(alt. Noelle)
French, meaning 'Christmas'.

Nola
Irish Gaelic, meaning 'white shoulder'.

Nona
Latin, meaning 'ninth'.

Nora
(alt. Norah)
Shortened form of Eleanor, meaning 'light'.

Noreen
(alt. Norine)
Irish, meaning 'light'.

Norma
Latin, meaning 'pattern'.

Normandie
(alt. Normandy)
French, from the province of the same name.

Novia
Latin, meaning 'new'.

Nuala
Irish Gaelic, meaning 'white shoulder'. Often refers to someone with white or very blonde hair.

Nydia
Latin, meaning 'nest'.

Nysa
(alt. Nyssa)
Greek, meaning 'ambition'.

N

Names of goddesses

Aphrodite (Love: Greek)
Demeter (Harvest: Greek)
Eos (Dawn: Greek)
Isis (Life: Egyptian)
Kali (Death: Indian)
Lakshmi (Wealth: Indian)
Minerva (Wisdom: Roman)
Nephthys (Death: Egyptian)
Saraswati (Arts: Indian)
Vesta (Hearth: Roman)

N

O Girls' names

Oceana
(alt. Ocean, Océane, Ocie)
Greek, meaning 'ocean'.

Octavia
Latin, meaning 'eighth'.

Oda
(alt. Odie)
Shortened form of Odessa,
meaning 'long voyage'.

Odele
(alt. Odell)
English, meaning 'woad hill'.

Odelia
Hebrew, meaning 'I will praise
the Lord'.

Odessa
Greek, meaning 'long
voyage'.

Odette
(alt. Odetta)
French, meaning 'wealthy'.

Odile
(alt. Odilia)
French, meaning 'prospers in
battle'.

Odina
Feminine form of Odin,
meaning 'creative inspiration',
from the Nordic god of the
same name.

Odyssey
Greek, meaning 'long
journey'.

Oksana
Russian, meaning 'praise to
God'.

Ola
(alt. Olie)
Greek, meaning 'man's defender'.

Olena
(alt. Olene)
Russian, meaning 'light'.

Olga
Russian, meaning 'holy'.

Olivia
(alt. Olivev, Oliviana, Olivié, Ollie)
Latin, meaning 'olive'.

Olwen
Welsh, meaning 'white footprint'.

Olympia
(alt. Olimpia)
Greek, meaning 'from Mount Olympus'.

Oma
(alt. Omie)
Arabic, meaning 'leader'.

Omyra
Latin, meaning 'scented oil'.

Ona
(alt. Onnie)
Shortened form of Oneida, meaning 'long awaited'.

Oneida
Native American, meaning 'long awaited'.

Onyx
Latin, meaning 'veined gem'.

Oona
Irish, meaning 'unity'.

Opal
Sanskrit, meaning 'gem'.

Ophelia
(alt. Ophélie)
Greek, meaning 'help'. Name of a doomed character in Shakespeare's *Hamlet*.

Oprah
Hebrew, meaning 'young deer'. Made popular by legendary TV host Oprah Winfrey.

Ora
Latin, meaning 'prayer'.

Orabela
Latin, meaning 'prayer'.

Oralie
(alt. Oralia)
French, meaning 'golden'.

Orane
French, meaning 'rising'.

Orchid
Greek, from the flower of the same name.

Oriana
(alt. Oriane)
Latin, meaning 'dawning'.

Color names

Blanche
Coral
Ebony
Fawn
Hazel
Olive
Rose
Scarlett
Sienna
Violet

Orla
(alt. Orlaith, Orly)
Irish Gaelic, meaning 'golden lady'.

Orlean
French, meaning 'plum'.

Orsa
(alt. Osia, Ossie)
Latin, meaning 'bear'.

Otthid
Greek, meaning 'prospers in battle'.

Ottilie
(alt. Ottie)
French, meaning 'prospers in battle'.

Ouida
French, meaning 'renowned in battle'.

Ozette
Native American, from the village of the same name.

Popular Scottish names for boys and girls

Aileen	Mac
Alastair	Malcolm
Angus	Rhona
Fergus	Rossalyn
Isla	Saundra

P Girls' names

Padma
Sanskrit, meaning 'lotus'.
Currently associated with TV
host Padma Lakshmi.

Paige
(alt. Page)
French, meaning 'serving
boy'.

Paisley
Scottish, from the town of the
same name.

Palma
(alt. Palmira)
Latin, meaning 'palm tree'.

Paloma
Spanish, meaning 'dove'.

Pamela
(alt. Pam, Pamala, Pamella)
Greek, meaning 'all honey'.

Pandora
Greek, meaning 'all gifted'.

Pangiota
Greek, meaning 'all is holy'.

Pansy
French, from the flower of the
same name.

Paradisa
(alt. Paradis)
Greek, meaning 'garden
orchard'.

Paris
(alt. Parisa)
Greek, from the mythological
hero of the same name. Also
the capital city of France.

Parker
English, meaning 'park keeper'.

P

Parthenia
Greek, meaning 'virginal'.

Parthenope
Greek, from the mythological
Siren of the same name.

Parvati
Sanskrit, meaning 'daughter of
the mountain'.

Pascale
French, meaning 'Easter'.

Patience
French, meaning 'the state of
being patient'.

Patricia
*(alt. Pat, Patrice, Patsy, Patti,
Pattie, Patty)*
Latin, meaning 'noble'.

Paula
Latin, meaning 'small'.

Pauline
(alt. Paulette, Paulina)
Latin, meaning 'small'.

Paxton
Latin, meaning 'peaceful town'.

Paz
Spanish, meaning 'peace'.

Pazia
Hebrew, meaning 'golden'.

> ## Gem and precious stone names
>
> Amber
> Crystal
> Diamond
> Emerald
> Garnet
> Jade
> Opal
> Pearl
> Ruby

Peace
English, meaning 'peace'.

Pearl
(alt. Pearle, Pearlie, Perla)
Latin, meaning 'pale gemstone'.

Peggy
(alt. Peggie)
Greek, meaning 'pearl'.

Pelia
Hebrew, meaning 'marvel of
God'.

Penelope
Greek, meaning 'bobbin
worker'. Penelope was also the
loyal wife of Odysseus in Greek
mythology.

Penny
(alt. Penni, Pennie)
Greek, meaning 'bobbin worker'.

Peony
Greek, from the flower of the same name.

Perdita
Latin, meaning 'lost'.

Peri
(alt. Perri)
Hebrew, meaning 'outcome'.

Perry
French, meaning 'pear tree'.

Persephone
Greek, meaning 'bringer of destruction'.

Petra
(alt. Petrina)
Greek, meaning 'rock'.

Petula
Latin, meaning 'to seek'.

Petunia
Greek, from the flower of the same name.

Peyton
(alt. Payton)
Old English, meaning 'fighting-man's estate'.

Phaedra
Greek, meaning 'bright'.

Philippa
Greek, meaning 'horse lover'.

Philomena
(alt. Philoma)
Greek, meaning 'loved one'.

Phoebe
Greek, meaning 'shining and brilliant'.

Phoenix
Greek, meaning 'red as blood'.

Phyllis
(alt. Phillia, Phyllida, Phylis)
Greek, meaning 'leafy bough'.

Pia
Latin, meaning 'pious'.

Pilar
Spanish, meaning 'pillar'.

Piper
English, meaning 'pipe player'.

Pippa
Shortened form of Philippa, meaning 'horse lover'.

Plum
Latin, from the fruit of the same name.

P

Spelling options

C vs K (Catherine or Katherine)
E vs I (Alex or Alix)
G vs J (Geri or Jerry)
N vs NE (Ann or Anne)
O vs OU (Honor or Honour)
S vs Z (Susie or Suzie)
Y vs IE (Carry or Carrie)

Polly
Hebrew, meaning 'bitter'.

Pomona
Latin, meaning 'apple'.

Poppy
Latin, from the flower of the same name.

Portia
(alt. Porsha)
Latin, meaning 'from the Portia clan'.

Posy
(alt. Posie)
English, meaning 'small flower'.

Precious
Latin, meaning 'of great worth'.

Priela
Hebrew, meaning 'fruit of God'.

Primrose
English, meaning 'first rose'.

Princess
English, meaning 'daughter of the monarch'.

Priscilla
(alt. Priscila)
Latin, meaning 'ancient'.

Priya
Hindi, meaning 'loved one'.

Prudence
Latin, meaning 'caution'.

Prudie
Shortened form of Prudence, meaning 'caution'.

Prunella
Latin, meaning 'small plum'.

Psyche
Greek, meaning 'breath'.

Popular names of English and Scottish Queens and Consorts

Anna	Mairi
Anne	Margaret
Catherine	Mary
Eleanor	Matilda
Elizabeth	Victoria

P

 Girls' names

Qiturah
Arabic, meaning 'incense'.

Queen
(alt. Queenie)
English, meaning 'queen'.

Quiana
American, meaning 'silky'.

Quincy
(alt. Quincey)
French, meaning 'estate of the fifth son'.

Quinn
(alt. Quinnie)
Irish Gaelic, meaning 'counsel'.

Foreign alternatives

Eleanor (Elenora, Elinor)
Helen (Galina, Helene)
Georgina (Jørgina)
Margaret (Gretel, Marguerite, Marjorie)
Sarah (Sara, Sarine, Zara)
Violet (Iolanthe)

No-nickname names

April	Jude
Beth	June
Dana	Karen
Joy	May

R Girls' names

Rachel
(alt. Rachael, Rachelle)
Hebrew, meaning 'ewe'.

Radhika
Sanskrit, meaning 'prosperous'.

Rae
(alt. Ray)
Shortened form of Rachel, meaning 'ewe'.

Rahima
Arabic, meaning 'compassionate'.

Raina
(alt. Rain, Raine, Rainey, Rayne)
Latin, meaning 'queen'.

Raissa
(alt. Raisa)
Yiddish, meaning 'rose'.

Raleigh
(alt. Rayleigh)
English, meaning 'meadow of roe deer'.

Rama
(alt. Ramey, Ramya)
Hebrew, meaning 'exalted'.

Ramona
(alt. Romona)
Spanish, meaning 'wise guardian'.

Rana
(alt. Rania, Rayna)
Arabic, meaning 'beautiful thing'.

Randy
(alt. Randi)
Shortened form of Miranda, meaning 'admirable'.

R

Rani
Sanskrit, meaning 'queen'.

Raphaela
(alt. Rafaela, Raffaella)
Spanish, meaning 'healing God'.

Raquel
(alt. Racquel)
Hebrew, meaning 'ewe'.

Rashida
Turkish, meaning 'righteous'. Made popular by comedy actress Rashida Jones.

Raven
(alt. Ravyn)
English, from the bird of the same name.

Razia
Arabic, meaning 'contented'.

Reagan
(alt. Reagen, Regan)
Irish Gaelic, meaning 'descendant of Riagán'.

Rebecca
(alt. Reba, Rebekah)
Hebrew, meaning 'joined'.

Reese
(alt. Reece)
Welsh, meaning 'fiery and zealous'.

Regina
Latin, meaning 'queen'.

Reina
(alt. Reyna, Rheyna)
Spanish, meaning 'queen'.

Rena
(alt. Reena, Rina)
Hebrew, meaning 'serene'.

Renata
Latin, meaning 'reborn'.

Rene
Greek, meaning 'peace'.

Renée
(alt. Renae)
French, meaning 'reborn'.

Renita
Latin, meaning 'resistant'.

Reshma
(alt. Resha)
Sanskrit, meaning 'silk'.

Reta
(alt. Retha, Retta)
Shortened form of Margaret, meaning 'pearl'.

Rhea
Greek, meaning 'earth'.

Rheta
Greek, meaning 'eloquent speaker'.

R

Rhiannon
(alt. Reanna, Rhian, Rhianna)
Welsh, meaning 'witch'.

Rhoda
Greek, meaning 'rose'.

Rhona
Nordic, meaning 'rough island'.

Rhonda
(alt. Ronda)
Welsh, meaning 'noisy'.

Ría
(alt. Rie, Riya)
Shortened form of Victoria, meaning 'victor'.

Ricki
(alt. Rieko, Rika, Rikki)
Shortened form of Frederica, meaning 'peaceful ruler'. Associated with TV host Ricki Lake.

Riley
Irish Gaelic, meaning 'courageous'.

Rilla
German, meaning 'small brook'.

Rima
Arabic, meaning 'antelope'.

Riona
Irish Gaelic, meaning 'like a queen'.

Ripley
English, meaning 'shouting man's meadow'.

Risa
Latin, meaning 'laughter'.

Rita
Shortened form of Margaret, meaning 'pearl'.

River
(alt. Riviera)
English, from the body of water of the same name.

Roberta
(alt. Robbie, Robi, Roby)
English, meaning 'bright fame'.

Robin
(alt. Robbin, Robyn)
English, meaning 'bright fame'.

Rochelle
(alt. Richelle, Rochel)
French, meaning 'little rock'.

Rogue
French, meaning 'beggar'. Rogue is also a key character in the comic book series *X-Men*.

Rohina
(alt. Rohini)
Sanskrit, meaning 'sandalwood'.

Roisin
Irish Gaelic, meaning 'little rose'.

Rolanda
German, meaning 'famous land'.

Roma
Italian, meaning 'Rome'.

Romaine
(alt. Romina)
French, meaning 'from Rome'.

Romola
(alt. Romilda, Romily)
Latin, meaning 'Roman woman'.

Romy
Shortened form of Rosemary, meaning 'dew of the sea'.

Rona
(alt. Ronia, Ronja, Ronna)
Nordic, meaning 'rough island'.

Ronnie
(alt. Roni)
English, meaning 'strong counsel'.

Rosa
Italian, meaning 'rose'.

Rosabel
(alt. Rosabella)
Contraction of Rose and Belle, meaning 'beautiful rose'.

Rosalie
(alt. Rosale, Rosalia, Rosalina)
French, meaning 'rose garden'.

Rosalind
(alt. Rosalinda)
Spanish, meaning 'pretty rose'.

Rosalyn
(alt. Rosaleen, Rosaline, Roselyn)
Contraction of Rose and Lynn, meaning 'pretty rose'.

Rosamond
(alt. Rosamund)
German, meaning 'renowned protector'.

'Powerful' names

Allura
Aubrey
Inga
Isis
Lenna
Ulrika

Rose
(alt. Rosie, Rosia)
Latin, from the flower of the same name. One of the most popular choices for middle names.

Roseanne
(alt. Rosana, Rosanna, Rosanne, Roseann, Roseanna)
Contraction of Rose and Anne, meaning 'graceful rose'.

Rosemary
(alt. Rosemarie)
Latin, meaning 'dew of the sea'.

Rosita
Spanish, meaning 'rose'.

Rowena
(alt. Rowan)
Welsh, meaning 'slender and fair'.

Roxanne
(alt. Roxana, Roxane, Roxanna, Roxie)
Persian, meaning 'dawn'. Made popular by the *Police* song.

Rubena
(alt. Rubina)
Hebrew, meaning 'behold, a son'.

Ruby
(alt. Rubi, Rubie)
English, meaning 'red gemstone'.

Ruth
(alt. Ruthe, Ruthie)
Hebrew, meaning 'friend and companion'.

Ryan
Gaelic, meaning 'little king'.

Popular South American names for boys and girls

Atl
Centehua
Citlali
Coatl
Eréndira
Itzli
Matlal
Teiuc
Xochitl
Zolin

R

S Girls' names

Saba
(alt. Sabah)
Greek, meaning 'from Sheba'.

Sabina
(alt. Sabine)
Latin, meaning 'from the Sabine tribe'.

Sabrina
Latin, meaning 'the River Severn'.

Sadie
(alt. Sade, Sadye)
Hebrew, meaning 'princess'.

Saffron
English, from the spice of the same name.

Safiya
Arabic, meaning 'sincere friend'.

Sage
(alt. Saga, Saige)
Latin, meaning 'wise and healthy'.

Sahara
Arabic, meaning 'desert'.

Sakura
Japanese, meaning 'cherry blossom'.

Sally
(alt. Sallie)
Hebrew, meaning 'princess'.

Salome
(alt. Salma)
Hebrew, meaning 'peace'. Supposedly given to seductresses or 'loose women'.

Samantha
(alt. Sam, Sammie, Sammy)
Hebrew, meaning 'told by God'.

Samara
(alt. Samaria, Samira)
Hebrew, meaning 'under God's rule'.

Sanaa
Arabic, meaning 'brilliance'.

Sandra
(alt. Saundra)
Shortened form of Alexandra, meaning 'defender of mankind'.

Sandy
(alt. Sandi)
Shortened form of Sandra, meaning 'defender of mankind'.

Sangeeta
Hindi, meaning 'musical'.

Sanna
(alt. Saniya, Sanne, Sanni)
Hebrew, meaning 'lily'.

Santana
(alt. Santina)
Spanish, meaning 'holy'.

Sapphire
(alt. Saphira)
Hebrew, meaning 'blue gemstone'.

Sarah
(alt. Sara, Sarai, Sariah)
Hebrew, meaning 'princess'.

Sasha
(alt. Sacha, Sascha)
Russian, meaning 'man's defender'.

Saskia
(alt. Saskie)
Dutch, meaning 'the Saxon people'.

Savannah
(alt. Savanah, Savanna, Savina)
Spanish, meaning 'treeless'.

Scarlett
(alt. Scarlet)
English, meaning 'scarlet'. Usually associated with the protagonist of Margaret Mitchell's novel Gone With The Wind, Scarlett O'Hara.

Scout
French, meaning 'to listen'. Taken from a lead character in Harper Lee's novel To Kill a Mockingbird.

Sedona
(alt. Sedonia, Sedna)
Spanish, from the city of the same name.

Selah
(alt. Sela)
Hebrew, meaning 'cliff'.

Selby
English, meaning 'manor village'.

S

Selena
(alt. *Salena, Salima, Salina, Selene, Selina*)
Greek, meaning 'moon goddess'.

Selma
German, meaning 'Godly helmet'.

Seneca
Native American, meaning 'from the Seneca tribe'.

Sephora
Hebrew, meaning 'bird'.

September
Latin, meaning 'seventh month'.

Seraphina
(alt. *Serafina, Seraphia, Seraphine*)
Hebrew, meaning 'ardent'.

Serena
(alt. *Sarina, Sereana*)
Latin, meaning 'tranquil'.

Serenity
Latin, meaning 'serene'.

Shakira
Arabic, meaning 'thankful'. Made popular by the Columbian singer.

Shania
(alt. *Shaina, Shana, Shaniya*)
Hebrew, meaning 'beautiful'.

Shanice
American, meaning 'from Africa'.

Shaniqua
(alt. *Shanika*)
African, meaning 'warrior princess'.

Shanna
English, meaning 'old'.

Shannon
(alt. *Shannan, Shanon*)
Irish Gaelic, meaning 'old and ancient'.

Shantal
(alt. *Shantel, Shantell*)
French, from the place of the same name.

Shanti
Hindi, meaning 'peaceful'.

Sharlene
German, meaning 'man'.

Sharon
(alt. *Sharen, Sharona, Sharron*)
Hebrew, meaning 'a plain'.

Shasta
American, from the mountain of the same name.

S

Spring names

April
Cerelia
Kelda
May
Primavera
Verda
Verna

Shauna
(alt. Shawna)
Irish, meaning 'the Lord is gracious'.

Shayla
(alt. Shaylie, Shayna, Sheyla)
Irish, meaning 'blind'.

Shea
Irish Gaelic, meaning 'from the fairy fort'.

Sheena
Irish, meaning 'the Lord is gracious'.

Sheila
(alt. Shelia, Shila)
Irish, meaning 'blind'.

Shelby
(alt. Shelba, Shelbie)
English, meaning 'estate on the ledge'.

Shelley
(alt. Shellie, Shelly)
English, meaning 'meadow on the ledge'.

Shenandoah
Native American, meaning 'after an Oneida chief'. Also the name of a national park.

Sheridan
Irish Gaelic, meaning 'wild man'.

Sherry
(alt. Sheri, Sherie, Sherri, Sherrie)
Shortened form of Sheryl, meaning 'man'.

Sheryl
(alt. Sherryl)
German, meaning 'man'.

Shiloh
Hebrew, meaning 'his gift'. From the Biblical place of the same name.

Shirley
(alt. Shirlee)
English, meaning 'bright meadow'.

Shivani
Sanskrit, meaning 'wife of Shiva'.

S

Shona
Irish Gaelic, meaning 'God is gracious'.

Shoshana
(alt. Shoshanna)
Hebrew, meaning 'lily'.

Shura
Russian, meaning 'man's defender'.

Sian
(alt. Sianna)
Welsh, meaning 'the Lord is gracious'.

Sibyl
(alt. Sybil)
Greek, meaning 'seer and oracle'.

Sidney
(alt. Sydney)
English, meaning 'from St Denis'. Sydney is also the Australian city.

Sidonie
(alt. Sidonia, Sidony)
Latin, meaning 'from Sidonia'.

Siena
(alt. Sienna)
Latin, from the town of the same name.

Sierra
Spanish, meaning 'saw'.

Signa
(alt. Signe)
Scandinavian, meaning 'victory'.

Sigrid
Nordic, meaning 'fair victory'.

Silja
Scandinavian, meaning 'blind'.

Simcha
Hebrew, meaning 'joy'.

Simone
(alt. Simona)
Hebrew, meaning 'listening intently'.

Sinead
Irish, meaning 'the Lord is gracious'.

Siobhan
Irish, meaning 'the Lord is gracious'.

Siren
(alt. Sirena)
Greek, meaning 'entangler'. In Greek mythology, sirens were beautiful and dangerous creatures who lured sailors to their deaths.

Siria
Spanish, meaning 'glowing'.

S

Skye
(alt. Sky)
Scottish, from the island of the same name.

Skyler
(alt. Skyla, Skylar)
Dutch, meaning 'giving shelter'.

Sloane
(alt. Sloan)
Irish Gaelic, meaning 'man of arms'.

Socorro
Spanish, meaning 'to aid'.

Sojourner
English, meaning 'temporary stay'.

Solana
Spanish, meaning 'sunlight'.

Solange
French, meaning 'with dignity'.

Soledad
Spanish, meaning 'solitude'.

Soleil
French, meaning 'sun'.

Solveig
Scandinavian, meaning 'woman of the house'.

Sonia
(alt. Sonja, Sonya)
Greek, meaning 'wisdom'.

Sophia
(alt. Sofia, Sofie, Sophie)
Greek, meaning 'wisdom'.

Sophronia
Greek, meaning 'sensible'.

Soraya
Persian, meaning 'princess'.

Sorcha
Irish Gaelic, meaning 'bright and shining'.

Sorrel
English, from the herb of the same name.

Spirit
Latin, meaning 'breath'.

Stacey
(alt. Stacie, Stacy)
Greek, meaning 'resurrection'.

Star
(alt. Starla, Starr)
English, meaning 'star'.

Stella
Latin, meaning 'star'.

S

Stephanie
(alt. Stefanie, Stephani, Stephany)
Greek, meaning 'crowned'. A consistently popular name for baby girls.

Sukey
(alt. Sukey, Sukie)
Shortened form of Susan, meaning 'lily'.

Sula
American, meaning 'peace' or 'little she-bear'.

Summer
English, from the season of the same name.

Sunday
English, meaning 'the first day'.

Sunny
(alt. Sun)
English, meaning 'of a pleasant temperament'.

Suri
Persian, meaning 'red rose'. Made popular by Tom Cruise and Katie Holmes, after the birth of their daughter.

Surya
Hindi, from the god of the same name.

Susan
(alt. Sue, Susann, Susie, Suzan, Suzy)
Hebrew, meaning 'lily'.

Susannah
(alt. Susanna, Susanne, Suzanna, Suzanne)
Hebrew, meaning 'lily'.

Svetlana
Russian, meaning 'star'.

Swanhild
Saxon, meaning 'battle swan'.

Sylvia
(alt. Silvia, Sylvie)
Latin, meaning 'from the forest'.

Summer names

August
June
Natsumi
Persephone
Soleil
Summer
Suvi

S

T Girls' names

Tabitha
(alt. Tabatha)
Aramaic, meaning 'gazelle'.

Tahira
Arabic, meaning 'virginal'.

Tai
Chinese, meaning 'big'.

Taima
(alt. Taina)
Native American, meaning
'peal of thunder'.

Talia
(alt. Tali)
Hebrew, meaning 'heaven's
dew'.

Taliesin
Welsh, meaning 'shining brow'.

Talise
(alt. Talisa, Talyse)
Native American, meaning
'lovely water'. Talisa Stark is
also a popular character on
HBO series Game of Thrones.

Talitha
Aramaic, meaning 'young
girl'.

Tallulah
(alt. Taliyah)
Native American, meaning
'leaping water'.

Tamara
(alt. Tamera)
Hebrew, meaning 'palm tree'.

Tamatha
(alt. Tametha)
American, meaning 'dear
Tammy'.

Tamika
(alt. Tameka)
American, meaning 'people'.

Tammy
(alt. Tami, Tammie)
Shortened form of Tamsin, meaning 'twin'.

Tamsin
Hebrew, meaning 'twin'.

Tanis
Spanish, meaning 'to make famous'.

Tanya
(alt. Tania, Tanya, Tonya)
Shortened form of Tatiana, meaning 'from the Tatius clan'.

Tara
(alt. Tahra, Tarah, Tera)
Irish Gaelic, meaning 'rocky hill'.

Tasha
(alt. Taisha, Tarsha)
Shortened form of Natasha, meaning 'Christmas'.

Tatiana
(alt. Tayana)
Russian, meaning 'from the Tatius clan'.

Tatum
English, meaning 'light-hearted'. Also the last name of American actor Channing Tatum.

Tawny
(alt. Tawanaa, Tawnee, Tawnya)
English, meaning 'golden brown'.

Taya
Greek, meaning 'poor one'.

Taylor
(alt. Tayler)
English, meaning 'tailor'.

Tea
Greek, meaning 'goddess'.

Teagan
(alt. Teague, Tegan)
Irish Gaelic, meaning 'poet'.

Teal
English, from the bird of the same name.

Tecla
Greek, meaning 'fame of God'.

Temperance
English, meaning 'virtue'.

Tempest
French, meaning 'storm'. Made popular by the Shakespeare play of the same name.

T

Teresa
(alt. Terese, Theresa, Therese)
Greek, meaning 'harvest'.

Terry
(alt. Teri, Terri, Terrie)
Shortened form of Teresa,
meaning 'harvest'.

Tessa
(alt. Tess, Tessie)
Shortened form of Teresa,
meaning 'harvest'.

Thais
Greek, from the mythological
heroine of the same name.

Thalia
Greek, meaning 'blooming'.

Thandi
(alt. Thana)
Arabic, meaning 'thanksgiving'.

Thea
Greek, meaning 'goddess'.

Theda
German, meaning 'people'.

Thelma
Greek, meaning 'will'.

Theodora
Greek, meaning 'gift of God'.

Theodosia
Greek, meaning 'gift of God'.

Thisbe
Greek, from the
mythological heroine of
the same name.

Thomasina
(alt. Thomasin, Thomasine,
Thomasyn)
Greek, meaning 'twin'.

Thora
Scandinavian, meaning 'Thor's
struggle'.

Tia
(alt. Tiana)
Spanish, meaning 'aunt'.

Tiara
Latin, meaning 'jewelled
headband'.

Tierney
Irish Gaelic, meaning 'Lord'.

Tierra
(alt. Tiera)
Spanish, meaning 'land'.

Tiffany
(alt. Tiffani, Tiffanie)
Greek, meaning 'God's
appearance'.

Tigris
(alt. Tiggy)
Irish Gaelic, meaning 'tiger'.

T

Tilda
Shortened form of Matilda, meaning 'battle-mighty'.

Tillie
(alt. Tilly)
Shortened form of Matilda, meaning 'battle-mighty'.

Timothea
Greek, meaning 'honoring God'.

Tina
(alt. Teena, Tena)
Shortened form of Christina, meaning 'anointed Christian'.

Tirion
Welsh, meaning 'kind and gentle'.

Tirzah
Hebrew, meaning 'pleasantness'. Also a biblical name.

Titania
Greek, meaning 'giant'.

Toby
(alt. Tobi)
Hebrew, meaning 'God is good'.

Toni
(alt. Tony)
Latin, meaning 'invaluable'.

Tonia
(alt. Tonja, Tonya)
Russian, meaning 'praiseworthy'.

Topaz
Latin, meaning 'golden gemstone'.

Tori
(alt. Tora)
Shortened form of Victoria, meaning 'victory'.

Tova
(alt. Tovah, Tove)
Hebrew, meaning 'good'.

Tracy
(alt. Tracey, Tracie)
Greek, meaning 'harvest'.

Treva
Welsh, meaning 'homestead'.

Tricia
Shortened form of Patricia, meaning 'aristocratic'.

Fall names

Autumn
Demetria
September
Theresa
Tracey

T

Trilby
English, meaning 'vocal trills'. Also the name of a style of men's hat.

Trina
(alt. Trena)
Greek, meaning 'pure'.

Trinity
Latin, meaning 'triad'.

Trisha
Shortened form of Patricia, meaning 'noble'.

Trista
Latin, meaning 'sad'.

Trixie
Shortened form of Beatrix, meaning 'bringer of gladness'.

Trudy
(alt. Tru, Trudie)
Shortened form of Gertrude, meaning 'strength of a spear'.

Tullia
Spanish, meaning 'bound for glory'.

Twyla
(alt. Twila)
American, meaning 'star'.

Tyler
English, meaning 'tiler'.

Tyra
Scandinavian, meaning 'Thor's struggle'. Associated with model Tyra Banks.

Tzipporah
Hebrew, meaning 'bird'.

Popular Spanish names for boys and girls

Carmen
Catalina
Diego
Esmeralda
Jesus
José
Juanita
Miguel
Ramona
Santiago

T

U

Girls' names

Ula
(alt. Ulla)
Celtic, meaning 'gem of the sea'.

Ulrika
(alt. Urica)
German, meaning 'power of the wolf'.

Uma
Sanskrit, meaning 'flax'.

Una
Latin, meaning 'one'.

Undine
Latin, meaning 'little wave'.

Unice
Greek, meaning 'victorious'.

Unique
Latin, meaning 'only one'.

Winter names

January
Neva
Neve
Perdita
Rainer
Tahoma

Unity
English, meaning 'oneness'.

Uriela
Hebrew, meaning 'God's light'.

Ursula
Latin, meaning 'little female bear'. One of the classic Disney villains, from *The Little Mermaid*.

Uta
German, meaning 'prospers in battle'.

V Girls' names

Vada
German, meaning 'famous ruler'.

Valencia
(alt. Valancy, Valarece)
Latin, meaning 'strong and healthy'.

Valentina
Latin, meaning 'strong and healthy'.

Valentine
Latin, from the saint of the same name.

Valerie
(alt. Valarie, Valeria, Valery, Valorie)
Latin, meaning 'to be healthy and strong'.

Valia
(alt. Vale, Vallie)
Shortened form of Valerie, meaning 'to be healthy and strong'.

Vandana
Sanskrit, meaning 'worship'.

Vanessa
(alt. Vanesa)
Greek, meaning 'butterfly'.

Vanity
Latin, meaning 'self-obsessed'.

Vashti
Persian, meaning 'beauty'.

Veda
Sanskrit, meaning 'knowledge and wisdom'.

Vega
Arabic, meaning 'falling vulture'.

Velda
German, meaning 'ruler'.

Vella
American, meaning 'beautiful'.

Velma
English, meaning 'determined protector'.

Venice
(alt. Venetia, Venita)
Latin, meaning 'city of canals'. From the Italian city of the same name.

Venus
Latin, from the Roman goddess of the same name. Venus was the goddess of love, beauty, sex and fertility.

Vera
(alt. Verla, Verlie)
Slavic, meaning 'faith'.

Verda
(alt. Verdie)
Latin, meaning 'spring-like'.

Verena
Latin, meaning 'true'.

Verity
Latin, meaning 'truth'.

Verna
(alt. Vernie)
Latin, meaning 'spring green'.

Verona
Latin, from the Italian city of the same name.

Veronica
(alt. Verica, Veronique)
Latin, meaning 'true image'.

Veruca
Latin, meaning 'wart'.

Vesta
Latin, from the Roman goddess of the same name.

Vicenta
Latin, meaning 'prevailing'.

Christmas names

Carol
Eve
Gloria
Holly
Ivy
Mary
Natasha
Noel
Robin

V

Victoria
(alt. Tori, Vicki, Vicky, Vikki, Vix)
Latin, meaning 'victory'. Often associated with Queen Victoria.

Vida
Spanish, meaning 'life'.

Vidya
Sanskrit, meaning 'knowledge'.

Vienna
Latin, from the city of the same name.

Vigdis
Scandinavian, meaning 'war goddess'.

Vina
(alt. Vena)
Spanish, meaning 'vineyard'.

Viola
Latin, meaning 'violet'.

Violet
(alt. Violetta)
Latin, meaning 'purple'.

Virginia
(alt. Virgie, Virginie)
Latin, meaning 'maiden'. Also the US state.

Vita
Latin, meaning 'life'.

Vittoria
Variation of Victoria, meaning 'victory'.

Viva
Latin, meaning 'alive'.

Viveca
Scandinavian, meaning 'war fortress'.

Vivian
(alt. Vivien, Vivienne)
Latin, meaning 'lively'.

Vonda
Czech, meaning 'from the tribe of Vandals'.

Food-inspired names

Anise
Candy
Cherry
Coco
Ginger
Honey
Meena
Olive
Saffron

Girls' names

Waleska
Polish, meaning 'beautiful'.

Wallis
English, meaning 'from Wales'. Often associated with Wallis Simpson, whose affair with King Edward VIII ultimately led to his abdication.

Wanda
(alt. Waneta, Wanita)
Slavic, meaning 'tribe of the vandals'.

Wava
English, meaning 'way'.

Waverly
(alt. Waverley)
Old English, meaning 'meadow of aspens'.

Wendy
English, meaning 'friend'.

Whisper
English, meaning 'whisper'.

Whitley
Old English, meaning 'white meadow'.

Whitney
Old English, meaning 'white island'.

Wilda
German, meaning 'willow tree'.

Wilhelmina
German, meaning 'determined'.

Willene
(alt. Willa, Willia)
German, meaning 'helmet'.

Willow
English, from the tree of the same name.

Wilma
German, meaning 'protection'.

Winifred
(alt. Winnie)
Old English, meaning 'holy and blessed'.

Winona
(alt. Wynona)
Indian, meaning 'first-born daughter'.

Winslow
English, meaning 'friend's hill'.

Winter
English, meaning 'winter', associated with the season.

Wisteria
English, meaning 'flower'.

Wren
English, meaning 'wren'.

Wynne
Welsh, meaning 'white'.

Bird names

Ava
Oriole
Raven
Teal
Wren

X Girls' names

Xanthe
Greek, meaning 'blonde'.

Xanthippe
Greek, meaning 'nagging'.

Xaverie
Greek, meaning 'bright'.

Xaviera
Arabic, meaning 'bright'.

Xena
(alt. Xenia)
Greek, meaning 'foreigner'.
Associated with the TV sci-fi
series of the same name.

Ximena
Greek, meaning 'listening'.

Xiomara
Spanish, meaning 'battle-
ready'.

Xochitl
Spanish, meaning 'flower'.

Xoey
Variation of Zoe, meaning
'life'.

Xristina
Variation of Christina, meaning
'follower of Christ'.

Xylia
(alt. Xylina, Xyloma)
Greek, meaning 'from the
woods'.

Popular Welsh names for boys and girls

Bronwen	Ioan
Cerys	Myfanwy
Dafydd	Owain
Dylan	Rhys
Gwynn	Siân

X

Y Girls' names

Yadira
Arabic, meaning 'worthy'.

Yael
Hebrew, meaning 'mountain goat'. Also a key figure in the Hebrew Bible.

Yaffa
(alt. Yahaira, Yajaira)
Hebrew, meaning 'lovely'.

Yamilet
Arabic, meaning 'beautiful'.

Yana
Hebrew, meaning 'the Lord is gracious'.

Yanira
Hawaiian, meaning 'pretty'.

Yareli
Latin, meaning 'golden'.

Yaretzi
(alt. Yaritza)
Hawaiian, meaning 'forever beloved'.

Yasmin
(alt. Yasmeen, Yasmina)
Persian, meaning 'jasmine flower'.

Yelena
Greek, meaning 'bright and chosen'.

Yesenia
Arabic, meaning 'flower'.

Yetta
English, from Henrietta, meaning 'ruler of the house'.

Yeva
Hebrew variant of Eve, meaning 'life'.

Ylva
Old Norse, meaning 'sea wolf'.

Yoki
(alt. Yoko)
Native American, meaning 'rain'. Usually associated with the artist and peace activist Yoko Ono.

Yolanda
(alt. Yolonda)
Spanish, meaning 'violet flower'.

Yoselin
English, meaning 'lovely'.

Yoshiko
Japanese, meaning 'good child'.

Ysabel
English, meaning 'God's promise'.

Ysanne
Contraction of Isabel and Anne, meaning 'pledged to God' and 'grace'.

Names from nature

Acacia
Amaryllis
Dahlia
Juniper
Primrose

Yuki
Japanese, meaning 'lucky'.

Yuliana
Latin, meaning 'youthful'.

Yuridia
Russian, meaning 'farmer'.

Yvette
(alt. Yvonne)
French, meaning 'yew'.

Z Girls' names

Zafira
Arabic, meaning 'successful'.

Zahara
(alt. Zahava, Zahra)
Arabic, meaning 'flowering and shining'.

Zaida
(alt. Zaide)
Arabic, meaning 'prosperous'.

Zalika
Swahili, meaning 'well born'.

Zaltana
Arabic, meaning 'high mountain'.

Zamia
Greek, meaning 'pine cone'.

Zaniyah
Arabic, meaning 'lily'.

Zara
(alt. Zaria, Zariah, Zora)
Arabic, meaning 'radiance'.

Zaya
(alt. Zayah)
Tibetan, meaning 'victorious woman'.

Zelda
German, meaning 'dark battle'. Made popular by the hugely successful video game series.

Zelia
(alt. Zella)
Scandinavian, meaning 'sunshine'.

Zelma
German, meaning 'helmet'.

Zemirah
Hebrew, meaning 'joyous melody'.

Zena
(alt. Zenia, Zina)
Greek, meaning 'hospitable'.

Zenaida
Greek, meaning 'the life of Zeus'.

Zenobia
Latin, meaning 'the life of Zeus'. Zenobia was also a Queen of ancient Roman Syria and led a famous revolt against the Romans.

Zetta
Italian, meaning 'Z'.

Zia
Arabic, meaning 'light and splendor'.

Zinaida
Greek, meaning 'belonging to Zeus'.

Zinnia
Latin, meaning 'flower'.

Zipporah
Hebrew, meaning 'bird'.

Zita
(alt. Ziva)
Spanish, meaning 'little girl'.

Zoe
(alt. Zoi, Zoie, Zoey, Zoeya)
Greek, meaning 'life'.

Zoila
Greek, meaning 'life'.

Zoraida
Spanish, meaning 'captivating woman'.

Zosia
(alt. Zosima)
Greek, meaning 'wisdom'.

Zoya
Greek, meaning 'life'.

Zula
African, meaning 'brilliant'.

Zuleika
Arabic, meaning 'fair and intelligent'.

Zulma
Arabic, meaning 'peace'.

Zuzana
Hebrew, meaning 'lily'.

Zuzu
Czech, meaning 'flower'.

Z